Cooking
for your
Freezer

Cooking
for your
Freezer
Mary Berry

Sundial

Contents

First published in 1977 by Sundial Books Limited
59 Grosvenor Street, London W1
Fifth impression, 1979
© 1977 Hennerwood Publications Limited
ISBN 0 904230 46 5
Printed in England by Severn Valley Press Limited

Introduction

In an age which has produced all manner of labour-saving devices, the freezer is an excellent addition to household equipment. Not only is it an extra food store, but also an aid to menu planning, a stand-by in emergencies and a money-saver. But it must, of course, be used properly.

Cooking for the freezer is just as important as buying for it. The casseroles, pies, home-made soups and sauces, the cakes, pastries, toddlers' dishes which can be kept in the freezer make it a remarkable asset in the kitchen. Preparing double the quantities—half for now and half for the freezer—ensures having meals for emergencies and saves time when you are busy.

It will help the household budget too, for doubling the quantity does not mean doubling the cooking time. The amount of energy required to cook, say, one stew is the same as for cooking two.

Another advantage of owning a freezer is being able to cook when it is convenient and time is available. How many people throw away chicken carcasses, for example, simply because there is not time to turn them into stock. They can however be wrapped and stored in the freezer until time is available to turn them into stock.

Packaging for the freezer

Packaging is more than just a means of keeping the contents of the freezer tidy and separate. It helps to preserve the quality of the food, prevents dehydration and loss of nutritional value, stops strongly flavoured foods from affecting others and inhibits bacteriological contamination between different items. For all these reasons, therefore, it pays to study the various methods of packaging carefully, decide which suits you best and buy accordingly.
Bags All freezer owners use some form of polythene bag. Bags are so useful, capable of moulding themselves around awkward shapes and holding liquid if required. They come in various sizes, some with gussets and some without, separated, on a roll, coloured and plain, and which you choose depends on the size of your family and how they will be used. Do buy the bags which are specially made for the freezer. They are thick enough to withstand the low temperature without splitting and if carefully washed and dried can be used again and again as a second wrap, but do not allow to contact food. Do not use bags supplied with clothes. Apart from the fact that they are not hygienic, they are also too thin to be satisfactory. *Boil-in-bags* are tough bags made to withstand being plunged straight from the freezer into boiling water. This

makes them particularly valuable if you have to go away leaving meals, mainly meat and fish in sauces, for those members of the family left at home. The dish can be prepared frozen, sealed in the bag, then heated without mess or bother. They are similar to the ones you buy containing cooked frozen meals. Other types of bag are made from aluminium foil, foil lined with plastic and paper lined with foil, and are bought with a strip seal.

Foil cases come in a great variety of shapes. Some have their own lids; others must be covered with foil. Their neat shapes make them particularly good for stacking. They are useful for complete meals, casseroles, pies and flans.

Rigid containers are usually supplied with lids and are ideal for liquids. The best are made of plastic and can be used in the larder or refrigerator as well as in the freezer. Their tops should fit well and make an effective seal. Buy them specially for the freezer, making certain they are suitable for use at low temperatures, otherwise the plastic can become brittle and will not last long. Waxed cartons are effective and if handled carefully can be re-used if relined with a polythene bag. However they are not suitable for hot liquids and food should be cooled before being packed in these containers.

Freezer-wrap is a see-through wrapping and is an alternative to foil. It must be secured by means of adhesive *freezer tape*. Ordinary adhesive tape will not seal in low temperatures.

Improvised containers Don't throw away old yogurt or margarine cartons, particularly if you have a baby or toddler to feed. Enough puréed vegetables, stewed fruits, etc., for one meal, fit very nicely into a small thoroughly washed carton if it is relined with a new plastic bag. Do not use cracked containers.

Twist-ties and other seals Twist-ties, usually made from paper covered wire, are supplied with polythene bags. If you like gadgets, you can get twist-tie dispensers in which the wire comes in a continuous reel and from which you cut off the amount you need. Alternatively, there are special machines for sealing bags with adhesive freezer tape—home versions of those used by butchers. Keen freezer cooks can buy electric bag sealers but they are quite expensive.

Organising the freezer

To be really efficient and economical, the contents of the freezer must be properly organised, so that you know where everything is and the items are used in strict rotation.

One of the best methods of storage involves grouping the same types of food together and always storing them in the same part of the freezer.

For really efficient storage it is possible to buy special stacking baskets which can be placed on the shelves of an upright freezer or stacked in the base of a chest freezer. Most chest freezers have room for three layers of baskets which helps to keep food organised in sections. Most chest freezers have one or more hanging baskets included in the purchase price. These can contain smaller articles, keeping like with like. Other baskets, some shallow, some deep, stacking or hanging, are available and enable you to make use of all the space in the freezer.

Colour-Coding While not essential, this is a sensible aid to freezer planning. By giving a different colour to each category of food and packing each item in an appropriately coloured bag or using coloured ties and labels, you can see at a glance where the meat or vegetables, the fish, fruit or pastries are.

Keeping a record Always keep a list of everything the freezer contains. This prevents items from remaining in the freezer for too long and enables you to plan a menu without removing the complete contents of the freezer to see what is available. It is possible to buy special record books with ruled columns for the item, date, quantity, etc. or you can use an exercise book and rule the columns yourself. Either way, see that it is kept near the freezer, together with a pencil or pen, so that entries can be made at once, or items crossed off as food is used.

Package shapes The freezer will run more cheaply and efficiently the less free space there is between packages and if it is kept well stocked. Obviously some things like joints are bound to be awkwardly shaped, but if possible try to freeze items into cubes or "brickets". Liquids, for example, can be poured into a polythene bag fitted inside an old sugar carton or square polythene box. When frozen, the carton "mould" can be removed. A casserole dish may be lined with foil and filled with stew to freeze. When frozen remove the dish and return it to the kitchen. Before heating, the stew can be thawed and reheated in the same dish.

Freezing food

Quality, speed and hygiene are the three watchwords of really successful freezer cooking.

Freezing won't make food *better* than it is when purchased so you should always use the best quality ingredients—young vegetables, fresh meat and fish—for best results. Speed—in cooling before freezing—limits the build up of harmful bacteria and prevents ice crystals from forming in the food, and spoiling its texture. Freezing in small quantities ensures rapid, even freezing. Hygiene is always important in the preparation of food, and food being cooked for the freezer is no exception. Very low temperatures do not destroy bacteria, they merely make them dormant and food that is contaminated before freezing will still be contaminated when thawed.

Packing food for the freezer Some dishes, such as casseroles or mince, can be frozen in a shallow meat-tin. When firm but not quite solid remove from tin, dipping the base quickly into hot water if necessary to free the contents, then cut. Wrap each block separately, seal and label and return to the freezer. Remove as much air from the package, smoothing it out with the fingers before sealing. Where possible use shallow containers rather than deep ones, so that the freezing process is quick and even.

Sealing and labelling An airtight seal is essential. Give the neck of a polythene bag a couple of twists before securing with a twist-tie or freezer tape. Labelling is equally important. Stick-on labels may be used, especially on foil, or you can write directly on to plastic bags with a permanent felt-tipped marker. Make certain the bag is dry.

The label should give as much information as possible since the contents of transparent packages look different when frozen. The quantity should be given—either by weight or the number of people it will feed. The date on which the food is frozen, or the date by which it must be used, should be shown. The dating method should be consistent and the family should be made familiar with it.

Fast freezing Most freezers, unless they are very

small, have a fast-freezing switch, which is manually operated. This over-rides the thermostat and allows the temperature within to drop below the normal running temperature of $-18°C$ ($0°F$), reaching $-28°$ to $-30°C$ ($-18°$ to $-22°F$). The lower the temperature the faster the food will freeze. The temperature drops throughout the whole cabinet but the coldest places will be near the sides where the freezing elements are situated. Chest freezers usually have a fast-freeze compartment with freezing elements in the dividing wall, and it is wise to keep this free from general storage. In upright freezers, the top or bottom shelf should be used, unless your model has a special fast-freeze shelf. The reason for having special compartments is to keep the un-frozen packs away from the remainder of the contents. Even when cooled, the newly prepared food will have the effect of raising the temperature of the items with which it comes into contact and even, temporarily, of the air within the fast-freeze compartment. This is why you should not try to freeze too much at any one time—the maximum amount is 10 per cent of the freezer's loading capacity in 24 hours. Remember to operate the fast-freeze switch before you plan to do any freezing as it takes two to three hours for the temperature to be reduced. It must be left on until the food is frozen all the way through, allowing about 2 hours for each $\frac{1}{2}$ kg (1 lb) of meat, poultry, fish, pies and cooked meals, or 1 hour for each $\frac{1}{2}$ kg (1 lb) of vegetables, fruit, liquids, cakes and bread. This is very approximate: naturally a deep thick parcel takes longer to freeze than a shallow thin one.

Open freezing This is a method of freezing food before it is packed. It is particularly convenient for food which would be a nuisance if frozen firmly together, such as vegetables, cakes, rissoles, fish cakes, etc. It is essential to open freeze items which squash easily, such as the decoration on iced cakes. Open freezing may be used to make storage easier. Garden peas, for example, can be divided into the amounts needed for a meal, packed in bags and frozen. With open freezing, however, the peas will be separated and, once frozen, will flow freely and can be packed into one bag and used in small quantities when needed. For open freezing, the items are spread on a special stacking open-freeze tray or on to a baking sheet lined with foil. They are packed into containers only when frozen solid.

Freezing vegetables

Only freeze vegetables which are young and freshly picked. Start by preparing them as if for immediate use. Always wash well.

All vegetables are better if they are blanched before freezing; that is, scalded briefly in boiling water. A blanching basket is usually recommended for the purpose, but I prefer a nylon muslin wine-straining bag bought from a home brewing shop. Using only a small quantity at a time, put the prepared vegetables into the bag or basket and lower into boiling water. Take the blanching time from the moment the water comes back to the boil. Each batch must be cooled before being packed into bags, sealed and labelled, and placed in the fast-freeze compartment for freezing. Cooling is carried out by immersing bag or basket in cold water to which you keep adding ice cubes. Alternatively, the vegetables can be put in a colander and cooled under running water. Cooling times are the same as blanching times.

Occasionally, if you have a glut of vegetables, it is possible to freeze without blanching. The results, however, should be eaten within two months as the enzymes present in the vegetables, which are inactivated by blanching, continue to be active at very low temperatures and will cause changes in colour, flavour and texture.
Blanching times The following is a guide to blanching times:

Asparagus—2–4 minutes; aubergines—4 minutes; whole French beans or thickly cut French beans—2 minutes; coarsely sliced runner beans—1 minute; broad beans—2 minutes; broccoli—3–4 minutes; brussels sprouts—3 minutes; carrots—3–5 minutes; cauliflower—3 minutes; celeriac—4 minutes; corn-on-the-cob—4–8 minutes; courgettes—1 minute; leeks—2–4 minutes; onions—2 minutes; parsnips—2 minutes; peas—1 minute; spinach—2 minutes; swedes—3 minutes; turnips—2 minutes. Mushrooms should be sautéed in butter, drained and cooled.

Freezing fruit

There are various ways of freezing fruit and much depends on how you intend to use it. Only freeze top quality fruit, just ripe. If over-ripe, purée first. Otherwise dry pack (freeze whole, without any additions), or stew gently, or prepare and either layer with sugar or cover with sugar syrup. Fruits such as peaches, apricots and pears, which are liable to discolour, should have ascorbic acid (Vitamin C) added to the cold syrup before freezing. The proportions: $\frac{1}{4} \times 5$ ml spoon ($\frac{1}{4}$ teaspoon) ascorbic acid to 600 ml (1 pint) syrup.

Thawing

Whether to thaw food or not, and how long dishes should be left to thaw, are two problems which puzzle people from time to time. Generally speaking most cooked foods are best thawed just before reheating—it saves fuel too. Food can be cooked from its frozen state, provided you remember to allow a longer cooking time, with a slightly lower temperature, and do not try to speed things up by increasing the heat. Vegetables, indeed, taste better if plunged into boiling water straight from the freezer.

Meat is best thawed before being roasted, but if you must cook meat from frozen, choose a joint with a bone in, allow 45 min. per $\frac{1}{2}$ kg (1 lb.) for beef and lamb at 180°C, 350°F, Gas Mark 4; 1 hr. per $\frac{1}{2}$ kg. (1 lb.) for pork at 200°C, 400°F, Gas Mark 6. It is advisable to have a meat thermometer to check that the inside of a joint is properly cooked. Raw poultry however *must* always be fully thawed before cooking so that it can cook quickly right through to the bone, thus ensuring the destruction of harmful bacteria which may be present. Some fruits, such as strawberries and raspberries, should not be thawed for too long as they tend to become soft and are much nicer while still slightly chilled.

Whatever you decide to thaw, it is best to allow the process to take place in the refrigerator overnight. If necessary, perhaps because you haven't given yourself enough time, food can be left to thaw at room temperature but cover well and do not allow to stand after thawing. A loaf of bread may be wrapped in foil and left to warm gently in the oven. Bread slices can be toasted from frozen.

Storage times

Cream and cream cheese containing less than 40 per cent butter fat separate when frozen. Double or whipping cream should be whipped for storing in the freezer.

Salad vegetables (lettuce, cucumber, etc.) will become limp and can only be frozen in the form of soups. Tomatoes may be frozen but will not afterwards be suitable for salads.

Whole eggs break in the freezer and if hard-boiled become rubbery. It is best to beat eggs for storage in the freezer.

Cooked whole boiled potatoes and spaghetti become soft in the freezer but roast potatoes and mashed potato toppings on such things as shepherd's pie and fish pies are quite successful.

Mayonnaise curdles after freezing.

Yogurt separates after freezing. Commercially frozen yogurt, however, contains a stabiliser. Plain yogurt freezes if you first add a tablespoon of honey.

Previously frozen food should not be re-frozen. Once thawed, it deteriorates more quickly than fresh food. That is to say, after a certain time its flavour and texture will begin to deteriorate although there will still be no danger to health. It can, however, be used for cooked dishes which are then frozen. If you want to serve food which is sure to be at its best, you should not exceed the storage times given in the column opposite:

Most vegetables—12 months raw mushrooms—1 month; cooked mushrooms —3 months; onions—3–6 months.
Most fruit including purées—12 months unstoned fruit—3 months; fruit pies—6 months.

Uncooked meats: lamb—6 months; pork—3 months; beef—8 months; mince, offal, tripe— 3 months; bacon, vacuum-packed—5 months; smoked bacon joints—2 months; unsmoked bacon joints—4 weeks; sausages—2 months.

Poultry etc.: chicken—12 months; duck— 6 months; giblets—2 months; game—6 months.

Fish: white—3 months; oily—2 months.

Cooked dishes: pies, casseroles, etc.—3 months.

Cakes, bread, pastry, etc.—6 months; sandwiches and scones—2 months; crisp bread and rolls—1 week; enriched bread, soft rolls— 4 months; breadcrumbs, croûtons—6 months; risen dough—2 weeks; unrisen dough—1 month; yeast—1 month.

Dairy produce: cream—3 months; eggs, unsalted butter—6 months; salted butter, cream with more than 35 per cent butter fat, hard cheese—3 months; cream cheese—6 weeks; Camembert, Brie cheeses freeze well—3 months.

All recipes serve four unless otherwise stated.
Cooking times given at the beginning of recipes apply only to cooking done before freezing. All instructions for cooking and serving after freezing are given at the end of recipes.

All spoon measurements are level.

Summer soup

Metric

1 bunch watercress
Outside leaves 2 lettuce
50 g butter
1 onion, peeled and sliced
*350 g potatoes, peeled
and sliced*
600 ml chicken stock
*Salt and freshly ground
black pepper*

Imperial

1 bunch watercress
Outside leaves 2 lettuce
2 oz butter
1 onion, peeled and sliced
*12 oz potatoes, peeled
and sliced*
1 pint chicken stock
*Salt and freshly ground
black pepper*

Cooking Time: 30 minutes

Milk and cream are added to the soup after thawing and reheating to prevent curdling.
Wash the watercress but do not remove the stalks, wash and roughly shred the lettuce. Melt the butter in a pan and gently cook the onion and potato for 5 minutes, without browning. Add the stock and seasoning, bring to the boil, cover and simmer for 15 minutes. Add the watercress and lettuce and simmer for a further 10 minutes, then purée through a sieve or in a blender.
To freeze: pour into a rigid container, cool, cover, label and freeze.
To cook and serve: thaw overnight in the refrigerator. Turn into a non-stick pan, then heat through, stir in 450 ml ($\frac{3}{4}$ pint) boiling milk and 150 ml ($\frac{1}{4}$ pint) single cream. Taste and adjust seasoning, garnish each serving with a sprig of watercress.

Beetroot soup

Metric

*450 g cooked beetroot,
skinned*
350 g potatoes, peeled
25 g butter
*1 small onion, peeled and
chopped*
1¼ litres chicken stock
*Salt and freshly ground
black pepper*

Imperial

*1 lb cooked beetroot,
skinned*
12 oz potatoes, peeled
1 oz butter
*1 small onion, peeled and
chopped*
2 pints chicken stock
*Salt and freshly ground
black pepper*

Cooking Time: about 50 minutes

Cut the beetroot and potatoes into large dice. Melt the butter in a large pan, add the onion, beetroot and potatoes and fry gently for about 5 minutes, stirring occasionally. Stir in the stock and seasoning and bring to the boil, then lower the heat and cover the pan. Simmer for 45 minutes, or until tender. Rub the soup through a sieve or purée in a blender.
To freeze: turn into a rigid container, cool, cover, label and freeze.
To serve: thaw overnight in the refrigerator. Turn into a saucepan and reheat gently. Taste and adjust seasoning. Serve piping hot. Stir a spoonful of thick cream into the centre of each serving if liked.

Chinese leaves and pepper soup

Metric

2 × 15 ml spoons oil
50 g butter
*225 g green peppers,
deseeded, cored and diced*
*2 onions, peeled and
chopped*
*½ head Chinese leaves,
shredded*
40 g flour
450 ml chicken stock
*Salt and freshly ground
black pepper*

Imperial

2 tablespoons oil
2 oz butter
*8 oz green peppers,
deseeded, cored and diced*
*2 onions, peeled and
chopped*
*½ head Chinese leaves,
shredded*
1½ oz flour
¾ pint chicken stock
*Salt and freshly ground
black pepper*

Cooking Time: 35 minutes

Heat the oil in a saucepan, then add the butter. When it has melted, add the peppers, onion and Chinese leaves and cook gently for 5 minutes. Blend in the flour and cook for 1 minute. Gradually stir in the stock and bring to the boil. Season and simmer, covered, for 30 minutes or until the vegetables are cooked. Sieve or blend the soup.
To freeze: turn into a rigid container, cool, cover, label and freeze.
To cook and serve: thaw overnight in the refrigerator. Turn the soup into a saucepan with 450 ml ($\frac{3}{4}$ pint) milk and heat through. Taste and adjust seasoning and just before serving, stir in 3 × 15 ml spoons (3 tablespoons) single cream.

Beetroot soup; Chinese leaves and pepper soup; Summer soup

Quick pea soup

Metric	Imperial
25 g bacon fat	1 oz bacon fat
3 large spring onions, peeled and chopped	3 large spring onions, peeled and chopped
Outside leaves of a lettuce, roughly shredded	Outside leaves of a lettuce, roughly shredded
450 g frozen peas	1 lb frozen peas
1 litre stock or water	1¾ pints stock or water
Salt and freshly ground black pepper	Salt and freshly ground black pepper

Cooking Time: about 10 minutes

Melt the bacon fat in a pan, add the spring onions and lettuce leaves and cook for 2 minutes. Add the peas, stock and seasoning, bring to the boil and simmer gently for about 5 minutes. Sieve, or purée in a blender.

To freeze: turn into a rigid container, cool, cover, label and freeze.

To serve: thaw overnight in the refrigerator. Place in a non-stick saucepan and reheat gently, taste and adjust seasoning, stir in 3 × 15 ml spoons (3 tablespoons) double cream and pour into bowls. If liked, garnish with croûtons.

Iced Spanish soup

Metric	Imperial
5 tomatoes, skinned and deseeded	5 tomatoes, skinned and deseeded
1 large onion, peeled	1 large onion, peeled
1 large green pepper, seeds and pith removed	1 large green pepper, seeds and pith removed
Half a cucumber	Half a cucumber
3 small cloves garlic	3 small cloves garlic
2 × 15 ml spoons chopped parsley	2 tablespoons chopped parsley
2 slices white bread without the crusts	2 slices white bread without the crusts
Salt and freshly ground black pepper	Salt and freshly ground black pepper
2 × 15 ml spoons wine vinegar	2 tablespoons wine vinegar
2 × 15 ml spoons oil	2 tablespoons oil
A few drops Tabasco sauce	A few drops Tabasco sauce
300 ml iced water	½ pint iced water

Make this soup when the tomatoes are at their most plentiful and cheap.

Place all the ingredients together to purée through a sieve or in a blender until smooth (place in the blender in two or three batches). Turn into a bowl and mix well.

To freeze: turn into a rigid container, cover, label and freeze.

To serve: thaw completely at room temperature, about 8 hours, stir thoroughly and spoon into serving bowls. Place an ice cube in the centre of each bowl. Serve very cold, with small separate bowls of chopped cucumber, onion, tomato, green pepper, and fried bread croûtons.

Leek and artichoke soup: Iced spanish soup

Leek and artichoke soup

Metric	Imperial
675 g Jerusalem artichokes	1½ lb Jerusalem artichokes
25 g butter	1 oz butter
225 g leeks, washed and sliced	8 oz leeks, washed and sliced
Scant litre stock	1½ pints stock
Salt and freshly ground black pepper	Salt and freshly ground black pepper
Bay leaf	Bay leaf

Cooking Time: about 50 minutes

Put the artichokes in a pan and cover with cold water, bring to the boil, cover and simmer for 15 minutes, then drain well and peel. Rinse out the pan and melt the butter in it, add the leeks and cook for 2 to 3 minutes, add the artichokes, stock, seasoning and bay leaf, cover and simmer for about 30 minutes. Remove the bay leaf and purée through a sieve or in a blender.

To freeze: turn into a rigid container, cool, cover, label and freeze.

To serve: thaw at room temperature for about 8 hours. Place in a saucepan with 300 ml (½ pint) milk and bring to the boil, stirring. Taste and adjust seasoning. Serve garnished with mint, if liked.

Vichyssoise

Metric	Imperial
675 g leeks	1½ lb leeks
50 g butter	2 oz butter
225 g onions, peeled and chopped	8 oz onions, peeled and chopped
450 g potatoes, peeled and diced	1 lb potatoes, peeled and diced
1¼ litres chicken stock	2 pints chicken stock
1 × 5 ml spoon salt	1 teaspoon salt
Freshly ground black pepper	Freshly ground black pepper

Cooking Time: about 1 hour

Trim the tops of the leeks to within 2.5 cm (1 in) of the white stem and cut off the roots. Slice lengthwise through the centre and wash thoroughly in cold water, shred. Melt the butter in a large pan, add the onion and the leeks, cover and cook gently for about 10 minutes. Add the potatoes and cook for another 10 minutes, then stir in the stock and seasoning, cover and simmer for 30 to 40 minutes. Purée the soup in a blender, or sieve. Taste and adjust seasoning, leave to cool.

To freeze: turn into a rigid container, cover, label and freeze.

To serve: thaw at room temperature for about 8 hours or overnight in the refrigerator. Turn into a saucepan, preferably non-stick, and reheat. Remove from heat, stir in 150 ml (¼ pint) double cream and sprinkle with parsley. For a special occasion, serve this soup cold – stir thoroughly when thawed, then stir in the cream and sprinkle with parsley, or a few snipped chives.
Serves 6

Quick pea soup; Vichyssoise

Farmhouse cheese straws

Metric

225 g flour
½ teaspoon salt
Pinch pepper
50 g butter
1 chicken stock cube
100 g Farmhouse English
Cheddar cheese, grated
50 g Parmesan cheese,
grated
2 egg yolks
Cold water

Imperial

8 oz flour
½ teaspoon salt
Pinch pepper
2 oz butter
1 chicken stock cube
4 oz Farmhouse English
Cheddar cheese, grated
2 oz Parmesan cheese,
grated
2 egg yolks
Cold water

Sieve the flour, salt and pepper into a bowl. Add the butter, cut into small pieces, with the crumbled stock cube and rub in until the flour resembles breadcrumbs. Add the cheeses with the egg yolks and stir well, add enough cold water to make a firm dough.

Roll out on a floured surface to 6 mm (¼ in) thickness. Trim the edges to make a neat square or rectangle then cut into straws each about 6 mm (¼ in) wide and 6.5 cm (2½ in) long. Re-roll the trimmings and cut out 6 or 8 circles about 7.5 cm (3 in) in diameter, then cut out the centres with a 5 cm (2 in) cutter to form rings.

To freeze: lay the straws and rings on a baking sheet or flat dish and open freeze. Pack in a rigid container, seal, label and return to freezer.

To cook: place on baking sheets and bake in a moderately hot oven (200°C, 400°F, Gas Mark 6) for 15 minutes or until golden brown. Cool on a wire rack for 10 minutes, then thread the straws through the rings.

Makes about 80

Party small ham quiches

Metric

For the pastry:
225 g flour
½ teaspoon salt
50 g butter
50 g lard
2 × 15 ml spoons cold
water

For the filling:
1 shallot, peeled and
chopped
15 g butter
100 g ham, finely chopped
75 g Gruyère cheese,
grated
2 eggs
6 × 15 ml spoons single
cream
2 × 5 ml chopped chives
Salt and freshly ground
black pepper

Imperial

For the pastry:
8 oz flour
½ teaspoon salt
2 oz butter
2 oz lard
2 tablespoons
water

For the filling:
1 shallot, peeled and
chopped
½ oz butter
4 oz ham, finely chopped
3 oz Gruyère cheese,
grated
2 eggs
6 tablespoons single
cream
2 teaspoons chopped chives
Salt and freshly ground
black pepper

Cooking Time: 40 minutes
Oven: 190°C, 375°F, Gas Mark 5
160°C, 325°F, Gas Mark 3

Make the pastry in the usual way (see Leek and Ham Flan, page 48). Roll out the dough on a floured surface and cut out 20 circles large enough to line deep patty tins. Press the circles into the tins, line them with greaseproof paper and dried beans and bake in the centre of a moderately hot oven for 15 minutes. Remove paper and beans. Reduce oven temperature to warm.

Place the shallot in a small pan with the butter and cook gently for about 5 minutes. Mix shallot with the ham and divide the mixture between the pastry cases, sprinkle a little cheese in each.

Blend together the eggs, cream, chives and seasoning, spoon the mixture into the cases.

Bake in a warm oven for about 20 minutes or until the filling is set. Remove from tins.

To freeze: cool, pack in a polythene bag, seal, label and freeze.

To serve: place in a moderate oven (180°C, 350°F, Gas Mark 4) for 15 to 20 minutes. Serve hot.

Farmhouse cheese straws; Party small ham quiches; Smoked haddock pâté

Smoked haddock pâté

Metric

450 g smoked haddock
fillet
50–75 g butter
3 × 15 ml spoons cold
water
15 g gelatine
150 ml double cream
150 ml single cream
3 hard-boiled eggs,
finely chopped
Salt and freshly ground
black pepper

Imperial

1 lb smoked haddock fillet

2–3 oz butter
3 tablespoons cold
water
½ oz gelatine
¼ pint double cream
¼ pint single cream
3 hard-boiled eggs, finely
chopped
Salt and freshly ground
black pepper

Line grill pan with foil, lay on the haddock fillet and dot with butter, grill on both sides under a medium grill for about 10 minutes or until the fish flakes easily. Remove the skin and any bones from the haddock and put in an electric blender with any cooking juices and the butter. Reduce to a purée and turn into a bowl. Put the water in a small bowl or cup and sprinkle on the gelatine. Leave to stand for 3 minutes to become spongey. Stand the bowl in a pan of simmering water and allow the gelatine to dissolve. Cool slightly and stir into the fish purée. Whisk the two creams together then fold in the fish purée and hard-boiled eggs. Season well and turn into a 900 ml (1½ pint) foil dish or terrine.
To freeze: Cool, cover and label, then freeze.
To serve: Thaw overnight in the refrigerator, turn out and garnish with tomato slices. Serve with hot French bread or toast.
Serves 6.

Scallops in shells

Metric	Imperial
100 g scallops	4 oz scallops
100 g haddock	4 oz haddock
150 ml milk or dry white wine	¼ pint milk or dry white wine
Slice of onion	Slice of onion
Sprig of parsley	Sprig of parsley
Bay leaf	Bay leaf
50 g butter	2 oz butter
50 g flour	2 oz flour
450 ml milk	¾ pint milk
50 g grated cheese	2 oz grated cheese
Salt and freshly ground black pepper	Salt and freshly ground black pepper
Mashed potato made with 675 g potatoes	Mashed potato made with 1½ lb potatoes

Cooking Time: about 15 minutes

Rinse and slice the scallops and leave the coral whole. Cut the haddock into small pieces and remove any skin and bone. Place the fish in a pan with the milk or wine, onion, parsley, bay leaf, bring to the boil, simmer for 5 minutes. Drain and keep the liquor on one side. Melt the butter, add the flour and cook for a minute, stir in the fish liquor and milk and bring to the boil, stirring. Add the cheese, scallops and haddock and season well.

Divide the fish sauce between 4–6 scallop shells, or individual ovenproof dishes, and pipe the mashed potato in a border around the edge of each dish.

To freeze: open freeze, then pack in polythene bags, seal and label and return to the freezer.

To cook: take from the freezer, remove the bags, and either cook at once in a hot oven (220°C, 425°F, Gas Mark 7) for about 1 hour, or thaw in the refrigerator for about 8 hours and then reheat in a hot oven for about 15 minutes.

Salmon and egg mousse

Metric	Imperial
15 g gelatine	½ oz gelatine
6 × 15 ml spoons water	6 tablespoons water
150 ml condensed consommé	¼ pint condensed consommé
175 g salmon	6 oz salmon
3 hard-boiled eggs	3 hard-boiled eggs
150 ml mayonnaise	¼ pint mayonnaise
150 ml double cream, whipped	¼ pint double cream, whipped
Salt and freshly ground black pepper	Salt and freshly ground black pepper
1 × 15 ml spoon chopped parsley	1 tablespoon chopped parsley

An ideal way of using up the last of the fresh salmon left over from a dinner party.

Put the gelatine in a bowl with the water, leave to soak for 5 minutes. Stand over a bowl of simmering water and stir until gelatine is dissolved. Add to undiluted consommé. Flake the salmon and remove any pieces of skin and bones. Finely chop the eggs, place in a bowl with the salmon, mayonnaise, cream and three-quarters of the consommé mixture and mix well together, taste and season.

Pour into a 1 l (1¾ pint) strong dish and leave until set. Add the parsley to the remaining consommé and pour over the mousse, leave until set.

To freeze: cover dish with foil, label and freeze.

To serve: thaw overnight in the refrigerator. Decorate with slices of hard-boiled egg.

Kipper mousse

Metric	Imperial
283 g packet buttered kipper fillets	10 oz packet buttered kipper fillets
300 ml double cream	½ pint double cream
2 × 15 ml spoons lemon juice	2 tablespoons lemon juice
Pinch cayenne pepper	Pinch cayenne pepper

Cook the kipper fillets as directed on the packet, remove them from the bag, drain off the butter and reserve it.

Remove all the dark skin and bones from the kipper fillets and pass through a sieve, or place them in a blender, with the cream, the reserved butter and the lemon juice. Blend until smooth, add cayenne pepper to taste.

Turn into 6 strong individual ramekin dishes.

To freeze: cover, label and freeze.

To serve: thaw overnight in the refrigerator. Garnish each dish with slices of stuffed olive and serve with hot toast.

Serves 6

Scallops in shells; Kipper mousse; Salmon and egg mousse; Taramasalata

Taramasalata

Metric

50 g crustless white bread
4 × 15 ml spoons cold milk
170 g jar smoked cod's roe
1 clove garlic, crushed
9 × 15 ml spoons oil
2 × 15 ml spoons lemon juice
Salt and freshly ground black pepper

Imperial

2 oz crustless white bread
4 tablespoons cold milk
6 oz jar smoked cod's roe
1 clove garlic, crushed
9 tablespoons oil
2 tablespoons lemon juice
Salt and freshly ground black pepper

Soak the bread in the milk and squeeze dry. Blend all the ingredients together, taste and adjust seasoning.

To freeze: turn into a small 300 ml (½ pint) foil dish, cover, label and freeze.

To serve: thaw overnight in the refrigerator, turn into a small dish and serve with lemon wedges and hot toast or French bread.

Avocado and onion dip

Metric	Imperial
2 avocados	2 avocados
75 g cream cheese	3 oz cream cheese
3 × 15 ml spoons lemon juice	3 tablespoons lemon juice
$\frac{1}{4}$ small onion, peeled and very finely chopped	$\frac{1}{4}$ small onion, peeled and very finely chopped
Freshly ground black pepper	Freshly ground black pepper

Cut the avocados in half and remove the stones, scoop out the flesh, put it in a bowl and mash well with a fork. Add the remaining ingredients and stir until well blended.
To freeze: place in a small rigid container, cover, label and freeze.
To serve: thaw at room temperature for 4 to 5 hours, turn into a bowl and serve with potato crisps, sticks of celery or carrot or small sausages.

Garlic bread

Metric	Imperial
2 cloves garlic	2 cloves garlic
$\frac{1}{2}$ teaspoon salt	$\frac{1}{2}$ teaspoon salt
Freshly ground black pepper	Freshly ground black pepper
100 g butter	4 oz butter
1 × 5 ml spoon chopped mixed herbs	1 teaspoon chopped mixed herbs
1 × 5 ml spoon chopped parsley	1 teaspoon chopped parsley
1 French loaf	1 French loaf

Crush the garlic with the salt to a smooth paste and put in a bowl with the pepper, butter and herbs. Cream well.
Cut the loaf along in 2.5 cm (1 in) slices to within 1.5 cm ($\frac{1}{2}$ in) of the bottom. Spread the slices on each side with the garlic butter and press together again. Wrap in foil.
To freeze: label and freeze.
To cook: thaw at room temperature for 3 to 4 hours, then heat in a moderately hot oven (200°C, 400°F, Gas Mark 6) for 12 to 15 minutes, still in foil, until hot and crisp.

Grapefruit and melon refresher

Metric	Imperial
1 small ripe melon	1 small ripe melon
1 grapefruit, peeled and segmented	1 grapefruit, peeled and segmented
2 × 15 ml spoons lime juice	2 tablespoons lime juice
50 g caster sugar	2 oz caster sugar

Halve the melon and remove the seeds. Peel the melon halves, cut the flesh into cubes and place in a rigid container with the grapefruit segments, lime juice and sugar. Leave to stand for 1 hour.
To freeze: cover, label and freeze.
To serve: thaw in the refrigerator overnight. Serve in 4 wine glasses.

Canadian style pâté

Metric	Imperial
450 g salt belly of pork	1 lb salt belly of pork
225 g lean pork	8 oz lean pork
100 g pigs' liver	4 oz pigs' liver
1 onion, peeled	1 onion, peeled
2 cloves garlic, crushed	2 cloves garlic, crushed
A little salt	A little salt
Freshly ground black pepper	Freshly ground black pepper
1 × 15 ml spoon chopped parsley	1 tablespoon chopped parsley
3 × 15 ml spoons sherry	3 tablespoons sherry
5 rashers Canadian style streaky bacon	5 rashers Canadian style streaky bacon

Cooking Time: 1$\frac{1}{2}$ to 2 hours
Oven: 160°C, 325°F, Gas Mark 3

Remove any rind and bones from the belly of pork and cut into small pieces, mince into a bowl with the lean pork, liver and onion. Add the garlic, seasoning, parsley and sherry, mix well together. Line the base and sides of a 1$\frac{1}{4}$ l (2 pint) ovenproof dish with bacon rashers, spread in the pork mixture, cover with a piece of foil, stand in a dish of water and bake in a warm oven for 1$\frac{1}{2}$ to 2 hours.
To freeze: cool completely, then cover casserole with a double thickness of foil, put in a polythene bag, seal, label and freeze.
To serve: thaw in the refrigerator overnight, or for 6 hours at room temperature. Serve with hot toast or French bread.

Grapefruit and melon refresher; Avocado and onion dip; Canadian style pâté; Garlic bread

Basic Scotch mince; Savoury mince pies; Cottage pie; Curry pies

Savoury mince pies

Metric

1 portion Scotch mince Shortcrust pastry made with 350 g flour (see page 48)

Imperial

1 portion Scotch mince Shortcrust pastry made with 12 oz flour (see page 48)

Place the mince in a bowl and make sure it is cold. Roll out two-thirds of the pastry and cut into six 14 cm (5½ in) circles and line six 10 cm (4 in) foil dishes. Roll out the remaining pastry and cut out six 10 cm (4 in) circles for lids. Divide the mince between the pies, damp the edges and cover with the lids. Flute the edges firmly with fingertips or the prongs of a fork or the tip of a round bladed knife. Decorate with pastry trimmings.

To freeze: wrap the pies individually in a double layer of foil, seal, label and freeze.

To cook: unwrap, glaze with milk or beaten egg, make a small slit in the centre of each pie and bake in a hot oven (220°C, 425°F, Gas Mark 7), for 25 to 30 minutes until golden brown.

Makes 6 individual pies

Cottage pie

Metric

*1 portion basic Scotch
mince*
*225 g carrots, peeled and
grated*
*1 × 15 ml spoon chopped
parsley*
*Salt and freshly ground
black pepper*
*450 g old potatoes, peeled
and boiled*
Knob of butter
A little milk

Imperial

*1 portion basic Scotch
mince*
*8 oz carrots, peeled and
grated*
*1 tablespoon chopped
parsley*
*Salt and freshly ground
black pepper*
*1 lb old potatoes, peeled
and boiled*
Knob of butter
A little milk

Combine the mince with the carrot and parsley, taste and
adjust seasoning. Turn into a pie dish. Sieve or mash the
potatoes, add the butter and milk, season to taste and pipe
over the top of the meat. Decorate with extra potato, if liked.
To freeze: open freeze, then wrap in foil, label and return
to freezer.
To cook and serve: remove wrapping and cook from
frozen in a moderately hot oven (200°C, 400°F, Gas Mark
6) for 1½ to 1¾ hours. Garnish with finely chopped parsley.

Basic Scotch mince

Metric

25 g dripping
*450 g onions, peeled and
chopped*
63 g can tomato purée
4 × 5 ml spoons salt
*Freshly ground black
pepper*
50 g flour
1 litre water
2 beef stock cubes
2 kg minced beef

Imperial

1 oz dripping
*1 lb onions, peeled and
chopped*
2¼ oz can tomato purée
4 teaspoons salt
*Freshly ground black
pepper*
2 oz flour
1¾ pints water
2 beef stock cubes
4 lb minced beef

Cooking Time: about 1 hour

Cook 2 kg (4 lb) mince at one go and pack in 4 lots. I do mine
in my meat roasting tin. This way, you can freeze until it is
almost solid, then turn it out like a jelly, leave until just (but
only just) thawed enough to cut into quarters, pack in
polythene bags, label and return at once to the freezer.
Heat the dripping in a large pan, add the onion, stir and fry
over a low heat until soft and lightly coloured. Stir in the
tomato purée, seasoning and flour and cook for 2 minutes.
Add the water and stock cubes with the mince and bring
to the boil, stirring. Cook gently, stirring occasionally, until
cooked through, about 30 to 45 minutes in a shallow pan
and an hour for a deeper pan.
Remove from heat and cool quickly.
To freeze: as suggested above or pack in 4 rigid containers,
or make into recipes and then freeze.
To serve: thaw and use as required.

Curry pies

Make as Savoury Mince Pies, but when putting the mince
in a bowl, stir in 1 teaspoon (or to taste) curry powder,
1 × 15 ml spoon (1 tablespoon) chutney and about 25 g (1 oz)
sultanas. Freeze, and bake as Savoury Mince Pies.
Makes 6 individual pies.

Italian meat balls

Metric

350 g sausagemeat
2 × 15 ml spoons oil
350 g onions, peeled and
sliced
1 clove garlic, crushed
4 sticks celery, scrubbed
and sliced
1 red pepper, deseeded
and sliced
3 × 15 ml spoons tomato
purée
300 ml cider or stock
100 g mushrooms,
cleaned and sliced
2 × 5 ml spoons sugar
Salt and freshly ground
black pepper
225 g noodles
100 g English Cheddar
cheese, grated

Imperial

12 oz sausagemeat
2 tablespoons oil
12 oz onions, peeled and
sliced
1 clove garlic, crushed
4 sticks celery, scrubbed
and sliced
1 red pepper, deseeded
and sliced
3 tablespoons tomato
purée
½ pint cider or stock
4 oz mushrooms,
cleaned and sliced
2 teaspoons sugar
Salt and freshly ground
black pepper
8 oz noodles
4 oz English Cheddar
cheese, grated

Cooking Time: about 30 minutes

Divide the sausagemeat into small pieces and roll into 24 small balls on a lightly floured surface. Heat the oil in a large pan and add the meat balls, onion and garlic and fry until brown. Add the celery, pepper, tomato purée, cider or stock and mushrooms and bring to the boil, add the sugar and seasoning. Simmer for 20 minutes. Cook the noodles as directed on the packet, drain well and stir into the sauce with the cheese. Taste and adjust seasoning. Turn into a rigid container.

To freeze: cool, cover, label and freeze.

To serve: thaw at room temperature for 8 hours, then turn into a casserole, cover and heat through in a moderate oven (180°C, 350°F, Gas Mark 4) for 1½ hours, stirring occasionally.

Beef Oxford

Metric	Imperial
1 kg stewing steak	2 lb stewing steak
40 g flour	1½ oz flour
50 g dripping	2 oz dripping
Salt and freshly ground black pepper	Salt and freshly ground black pepper
225 g onions, peeled and sliced	8 oz onions, peeled and sliced
2 cloves garlic, crushed	2 cloves garlic, crushed
100 g mushrooms, cleaned and sliced	4 oz mushrooms, cleaned and sliced
1 green pepper, deseeded and sliced	1 green pepper, deseeded and sliced
2 × 15 ml spoons apricot jam	2 tablespoons apricot jam
300 ml red wine	½ pint red wine
300 ml beef stock	½ pint beef stock

Cooking Time: 2–2½ hours

Cut the meat into neat pieces, put in a polythene bag with the flour and toss until well coated. Melt the dripping in a pan and fry the meat quickly to brown. Add all the remaining ingredients, including any flour left in the bag, bring to the boil, cover and simmer for 2 to 2½ hours or until the meat is tender, stirring occasionally.

To freeze: turn into a rigid container, cool, cover, label and freeze.

To serve: thaw overnight in the refrigerator, place in a saucepan and reheat gently, stirring until piping hot.

Serves 6

Italian meat balls; Beef Oxford

Meat balls in sweet and sour sauce

Metric

350 g minced beef
50 g fresh white
breadcrumbs
1 egg
Salt and freshly ground
black pepper
2 × 15 ml spoons oil
1 onion, peeled and finely
chopped
2 carrots, peeled and cut
into long strips
1 leek, washed and finely
sliced
2 sticks celery, scrubbed
and finely sliced
4 × 5 ml spoons cornflour
2 × 5 ml spoons sugar
300 ml water
2 × 15 ml spoons tomato
ketchup
1 × 15 ml spoon vinegar
1 × 15 ml spoon soy sauce

Imperial

12 oz minced beef
2 oz fresh white
breadcrumbs
1 egg
Salt and freshly ground
black pepper
2 tablespoons oil
1 onion, peeled and finely
chopped
2 carrots, peeled and cut
into long strips
1 leek, washed and finely
sliced
2 sticks celery, scrubbed
and finely sliced
4 teaspoons cornflour
2 teaspoons sugar
½ pint water
2 tablespoons tomato
ketchup
1 tablespoon vinegar
1 tablespoon soy sauce

Cooking Time: 40 minutes

Place the minced beef, breadcrumbs, egg and seasoning together in a bowl and mix well. Turn on to a floured board and shape into 16 meat balls. Heat the oil in a pan and fry the meat balls until brown all over, lift on to a plate. Add the onion, carrot, leek and celery to the pan and fry slowly. Place the cornflour and sugar in a bowl and gradually stir in the water, add the ketchup, vinegar and soy sauce, pour into the pan and bring to the boil, stirring. Return the meat balls to the pan, cover with a lid and simmer for 30 minutes.
To freeze: turn into a rigid container, cool, cover, label and freeze.
To serve: thaw at room temperature for 4 to 5 hours, turn into a saucepan and heat through gently. Serve if liked with ribbon noodles.

Spaghetti sauce

Metric

450 g lean mince
A little dripping
1 rasher streaky bacon,
chopped
15 g flour
3 sticks celery, scrubbed
and chopped
225 g onions, peeled and
chopped
300 ml water
1 clove garlic, crushed
1 beef stock cube
Salt and freshly ground
black pepper
¼ teaspoon dried herbs
85 g concentrated
tomato purée
25 g Spanish stuffed green
olives, sliced

Imperial

1 lb lean mince
A little dripping
1 rasher streaky bacon,
chopped
½ oz flour
3 sticks celery, scrubbed
and chopped
8 oz onions, peeled and
chopped
½ pint water
1 clove garlic, crushed
1 beef stock cube
Salt and freshly ground
black pepper
¼ teaspoon dried herbs
3½ oz concentrated
tomato purée
1 oz Spanish stuffed green
olives, sliced

Cooking Time: 1¾ hours

Place the mince and dripping in a pan with the bacon and cook slowly until the fat has run out, then brown, turning frequently. Add the flour and blend well. Stir in all the other ingredients, except the olives, bring to the boil, cover and simmer for about 1 hour or until tender. Add the olives and taste and adjust seasoning.
To freeze: turn into a rigid container, cool, cover, label and freeze.
To serve: thaw overnight in the refrigerator or at room temperature for about 6 hours, turn into a saucepan and reheat gently. Serve with spaghetti.

European lasagne; Meat balls in sweet and sour sauce; Spaghetti sauce

European lasagne

Metric	Imperial
45 g butter	1¾ oz butter
40 g flour	1½ oz flour
600 ml milk	1 pint milk
¼ teaspoon made mustard	¼ teaspoon made mustard
A little ground nutmeg	A little ground nutmeg
¼ teaspoon salt	¼ teaspoon salt
100 g English Cheddar cheese, grated	4 oz English Cheddar cheese, grated
50 g Gruyère cheese, grated	2 oz Gruyère cheese, grated
15 g Parmesan cheese, grated	½ oz Parmesan cheese, grated
1 quantity Spaghetti sauce (see opposite)	1 quantity Spaghetti sauce (see opposite)
150 g lasagne	5 oz lasagne

To make the white sauce, melt the butter in a pan, add the flour and cook for 1 minute. Add the milk and bring to the boil, stirring, add the mustard, nutmeg and salt. Take a 23 cm (9 in) square foil dish or 2 l (3½ pint) shallow ovenproof casserole, and put in a layer of white sauce, then cheese, meat sauce and raw lasagne. Repeat and finish with a final layer of white sauce and cheese. Do not overlap the lasagne, break the pieces if necessary to fit the dish.

To freeze: leave until cold, cover, label and freeze.

To cook: thaw for 24 hours in the refrigerator, or 12 hours at room temperature. Remove the lid and cook in a moderately hot oven (190°C, 375°F, Gas Mark 5) for about ¾ to 1 hour, until golden brown. Allow an extra ½ to ¾ hour if using an ovenproof casserole.

Note: the sauces are more runny than usual to allow the raw pasta to cook and absorb the liquid.

Serves 5 to 6 portions

Beef curry

Metric	Imperial
1 kg stewing beef	*2 lb stewing beef*
40 g flour	*1½ oz flour*
1½ × 5 ml spoons salt	*1½ teaspoons salt*
1 large onion, peeled and chopped	*1 large onion, peeled and chopped*
50 g margarine	*2 oz margarine*
3 × 5 ml spoons curry powder	*3 teaspoons curry powder*
1 × 15 ml spoon paprika	*1 tablespoon paprika*
300 ml beef stock	*½ pint beef stock*
2 dried red chillies	*2 dried red chillies*
1 × 15 ml spoon mango chutney	*1 tablespoon mango chutney*
1 × 5 ml spoon Worcestershire sauce	*1 teaspoon Worcestershire sauce*
454 g can pineapple cubes	*1 lb can pineapple cubes*
2 bay leaves	*2 bay leaves*

Cooking Time: 1¾ hours

Cut the beef into 2 cm (¾ in) cubes and toss in the flour and salt.

Put the onion in a pan with the margarine and fry until soft, stir in the curry powder and paprika, fry for 2 minutes then add the beef, stir well and cook for 5 minutes.

Add the remaining ingredients to the pan, including the pineapple syrup. Cover and cook gently for 1½ hours or until tender.

Remove the bay leaves and chillies and taste and adjust the seasoning.

To freeze: cool, turn into a rigid container, cover, label and freeze.

To serve: thaw overnight in the refrigerator or for 6 to 8 hours at room temperature. Turn into a casserole and heat through in a moderate oven (180°C, 350°F, Gas Mark 4) for 45 minutes. Serve with boiled rice.

Steak and kidney pies

Metric	Imperial
225 g stewing steak	*8 oz stewing steak*
225 g ox kidney	*8 oz ox kidney*
40 g flour	*1½ oz flour*
25 g dripping	*1 oz dripping*
1 large onion, peeled and chopped	*1 large onion, peeled and chopped*
300 ml beef stock	*½ pint beef stock*
Salt and freshly ground black pepper	*Salt and freshly ground black pepper*
100 g mushrooms, cleaned and sliced	*4 oz mushrooms, cleaned and sliced*
Shortcrust pastry made with 350 g flour (see page 48)	*Shortcrust pastry made with 12 oz flour (see page 48)*

Cooking Time: 1½ hours

Cut the meat and kidney into 1.5 cm (½ in) cubes and toss in the flour. Heat the dripping in a pan, add the onion and fry for 2 to 3 minutes. Add the meat and kidney and fry until browned. Stir in the stock and seasoning and bring to the boil, partially cover and simmer for 1¼ hours. Add the mushrooms and cook for a further 15 minutes. Taste and adjust seasoning and leave to cool.

Roll out two-thirds of the pastry and cut into six 14 cm (5½ in) circles and line six 10 cm (4 in) foil dishes. Roll out the remaining pastry and cut six 10 cm (4 in) circles for lids. Divide the filling between the pies. Dampen the edges and cover with the lids. Seal the edges firmly with the prongs of a fork or the tip of a round bladed knife.

To freeze: cool and wrap each pie individually in a double layer of foil, label and freeze.

To serve: unwrap, glaze with milk or beaten egg, make a small slit in the centre of each pie. If liked, put into oven-proof dishes, and bake in a hot oven (220°C, 425°F, Gas Mark 7) for 25 to 30 minutes until golden brown.

Makes 6 individual pies

Beef curry; Hot spiced pancakes; Steak and kidney pies

Hot spiced pancakes

Metric

A little dripping
350 g mince
25 g flour
¼ teaspoon Tabasco sauce
¼ teaspoon ground ginger
Salt
226 g can tomatoes
1 clove garlic, crushed
1 × 5 ml spoon
Worcestershire sauce
1 × 5 ml spoon wine
vinegar
8 pancakes (see page 55)

Cheese sauce:
25 g butter
25 g flour
300 ml milk
50 g Cheddar cheese,
grated
1 × 5 ml spoon made
mustard
Salt and freshly ground
black pepper

Imperial

A little dripping
12 oz mince
1 oz flour
¼ teaspoon Tabasco sauce
¼ teaspoon ground ginger
Salt
8 oz can tomatoes
1 clove garlic, crushed
1 teaspoon
Worcestershire sauce
1 teaspoon wine
vinegar
8 pancakes (see page 55)

Cheese sauce:
1 oz butter
1 oz flour
½ pint milk
2 oz Cheddar cheese,
grated
1 teaspoon made
mustard
Salt and freshly ground
black pepper

Cooking Time: 1 hour

Melt the dripping in a pan and add the mince, fry, stirring, for 3 to 4 minutes until any fat runs out. Add the flour and cook for 1 minute, add Tabasco sauce, ginger, salt, tomatoes, garlic, Worcestershire sauce and vinegar, bring to the boil, cover, reduce the heat and simmer for 45 minutes until cooked. Taste and adjust seasoning, leave to cool.

Divide the filling between the pancakes and roll up, lay in a single layer in a foil dish.

To make the cheese sauce, melt the butter in a pan and stir in the flour, cook for 1 minute, add the milk and bring to the boil, stirring. Simmer until thickened then stir in the cheese, mustard and seasoning. Pour over the pancakes and leave to cool.

To freeze: cover, label and freeze.

To serve: thaw in the refrigerator overnight, remove the lid, sprinkle with 50 g (2 oz) grated Cheddar cheese and bake in a moderately hot oven (200°C, 400°F, Gas Mark 6) for 30 minutes, until golden brown. Serve with a salad.

Moussaka

Metric	Imperial	Cooking Time: 25 minutes
4 large aubergines	4 large aubergines	Slice the aubergines, sprinkle with salt and leave for 30 minutes. Drain and dry on kitchen paper. Fry the slices in 6 × 15 ml spoons (6 tablespoons) oil until brown on both sides. Remove from the pan and drain. Put the remaining oil in the pan with the lamb and brown. Add the onion and cook for 10 minutes. Blend in the flour, garlic, tomatoes and herbs, bring to the boil and taste and adjust seasoning. Arrange the aubergine slices and lamb mixture in layers in a buttered shallow ovenproof dish. Pour over the cheese sauce and sprinkle with the extra cheese. Cool.
Salt	Salt	
7 × 15 ml spoons oil	7 tablespoons oil	
450 g minced lamb	1 lb minced lamb	
225 g onions, peeled and chopped	8 oz onions, peeled and chopped	
25 g flour	1 oz flour	
1 clove garlic, crushed	1 clove garlic, crushed	
396 g can tomatoes	14 oz can tomatoes	
¼ teaspoon dried mixed herbs	¼ teaspoon dried mixed herbs	
2 × 15 ml spoons chopped parsley	2 tablespoons chopped parsley	To freeze: open freeze, remove from the dish, put in a polythene bag, seal, label and return to freezer.
Freshly ground black pepper	Freshly ground black pepper	To serve: remove plastic bag, return the moussaka to the dish and reheat in a moderately hot oven (200°C, 400°F, Gas Mark 6) for 1 hour.
300 ml cheese sauce (see page 29)	½ pint cheese sauce (see page 29)	
50 g grated Cheddar cheese	2 oz grated Cheddar cheese	

Creamed pork

Metric	Imperial	Cooking Time: 1 hour
450 g pork fillet	1 lb pork fillet	Cut the pork into 1.5 cm (½ in) slices. Melt the butter in a pan, add the pork and fry quickly for 3 to 4 minutes to seal the juices, remove the pork and put on one side. Stir the flour into the butter in the pan and cook for 1 minute. Add the stock and bring to the boil, stirring, return the pork to the pan. Cut the carrots in quarters lengthwise, add to the pan with the seasoning, cover and simmer for 45 minutes. Add the mushrooms and cook for a further 15 minutes.
40 g butter	1½ oz butter	
50 g flour	2 oz flour	
600 ml stock	1 pint stock	
225 g small carrots, peeled	8 oz small carrots, peeled	
Salt and freshly ground black pepper	Salt and freshly ground black pepper	To freeze: cool, turn into a rigid container, cover, freeze.
100 g button mushrooms, cleaned	4 oz button mushrooms, cleaned	To serve: thaw overnight in the refrigerator, turn into a saucepan and reheat gently, stirring occasionally, bring to the boil. Just before serving remove pan from the heat and stir in 150 ml (¼ pint) single cream, turn into a dish.

Lamb steaks in piquant sauce

Metric	Imperial	Cooking Time: ¾ to 1 hour
50 g butter	2 oz butter	Place the butter in a small pan and fry the onion and garlic for 5 minutes until golden brown. Stir in the flour and cook for 1 minute. Add the can of tomatoes, tomato purée, sugar, paprika and vinegar and cook together for 3 to 4 minutes. Taste and adjust seasoning. Lay the lamb in a shallow ovenproof dish and pour over the sauce. Cover and bake for ¾ to 1 hour until the lamb is tender.
1 large onion, peeled and chopped	1 large onion, peeled and chopped	
1 clove garlic, crushed	1 clove garlic, crushed	
15 g flour	½ oz flour	
396 g can tomatoes	14 oz can tomatoes	
1 × 15 ml spoon tomato purée	1 tablespoon tomato purée	
1 × 15 ml spoon brown sugar	1 tablespoon brown sugar	To freeze: cool quickly, cover, label and freeze.
¼ teaspoon paprika	¼ teaspoon paprika	To serve: thaw at room temperature for 6 hours then reheat in a moderate oven (180°C, 350°F, Gas Mark 4) for 45 minutes.
3 × 15 ml spoons vinegar	3 tablespoons vinegar	
Salt and freshly ground black pepper	Salt and freshly ground black pepper	
4 lamb leg steaks	4 lamb leg steaks	

Lamb steaks in piquant sauce; Spiced pork rolls; Creamed pork; Moussaka

Spiced pork rolls

Metric

225 g pork sausagemeat
Finely grated rind of ½
lemon
2 × 5 ml spoons chopped
mixed fresh herbs
4 pork escalopes
2 × 15 ml spoons oil
25 g butter
1 onion, peeled and
chopped
1 × 15 ml spoon paprika
1 × 15 ml spoon flour
300 ml stock
5 × 15 ml spoons sherry
1 × 5 ml spoon tomato
purée
Salt and freshly ground
black pepper
175 g button mushrooms,
cleaned

Imperial

8 oz pork sausagemeat
Finely grated rind of ½
lemon
2 teaspoons chopped
mixed fresh herbs
4 pork escalopes
2 tablespoons oil
1 oz butter
1 onion, peeled and
chopped
1 tablespoon paprika
1 tablespoon flour
½ pint stock
5 tablespoons sherry
1 teaspoon tomato
purée
Salt and freshly ground
black pepper
6 oz button mushrooms,
cleaned

Cooking Time: about 45 minutes

Mix the sausagemeat with the lemon rind and herbs, divide the mixture between the escalopes, spread flat then roll up and secure with two pieces of string or wooden cocktail sticks. Fry quickly in the oil and butter until just beginning to brown, then remove from the pan.

Add the onion and paprika to the pan and cook for 3 minutes, stir in the flour, remove the pan from the heat and stir in the stock, sherry and tomato purée. Return to the heat and bring to the boil, stirring, simmer until the sauce has thickened.

Add the pork rolls to the pan with seasoning, cover and simmer for 45 minutes or until tender. Stir in the mushrooms and cook for 2 to 3 minutes.

To freeze: remove the string or cocktail sticks from the pork rolls, then turn into a rigid container, cool, cover, label and freeze.

To serve: thaw overnight in the refrigerator. Place in a saucepan and reheat gently until piping hot, remove the pan from the heat and stir in 150 ml (¼ pint) soured cream just before serving.

31

Frugal Irish stew

Frugal Irish stew

Metric	Imperial
Large breast of lamb, on the bone	Large breast of lamb, on the bone
450 g onions, peeled and sliced	1 lb onions, peeled and sliced
1 kg potatoes, peeled and sliced	2 lb potatoes, peeled and sliced
Salt and freshly ground black pepper	Salt and freshly ground black pepper
225 g carrots, peeled and sliced	8 oz carrots, peeled and sliced
1 × 5 ml spoon chopped fresh thyme or ½ teaspoon dried	1 teaspoon chopped fresh thyme or ½ teaspoon dried
Water	Water

Cooking Time: 2 hours
Oven: 160°C, 325°F, Gas Mark 3

Cut the lamb into neat serving pieces and trim off any excess fat.

Put half the onion into a 1¾ l (3 pint) casserole, add half the potato and then the meat, seasoning each layer well. Cover with the carrots, then add the remaining onion and finish with a layer of potato. Add the thyme and enough water to come half way up the casserole.

Cover and cook in a warm oven for 1 hour, then remove the lid and cook for a further hour.

To freeze: cool quickly, cover, label and freeze.

To serve: thaw completely overnight in the refrigerator, then reheat in a moderate oven (180°C, 350°F, Gas Mark 4) for about 1½ hours, until hot through.

Lamb with Spanish rice stuffing

Lamb with Spanish rice stuffing

Metric

141 g packet Spanish rice
1½ kg boned shoulder of
English, Scotch or Welsh
lamb
A little marjoram
25 g dripping
1 × 15 ml spoon flour
300 ml stock
1 × 15 ml spoon tomato
purée
Salt and freshly ground
black pepper

Imperial

5 oz packet Spanish rice
3 lb boned shoulder of
English, Scotch or Welsh
lamb
A little marjoram
1 oz dripping
1 tablespoon flour
½ pint stock
1 tablespoon tomato
purée
Salt and freshly ground
black pepper

Cook the rice according to the directions on the packet. Remove from the heat and leave to cool.
To freeze: place the meat in a polythene bag, seal, label and freeze. Place the rice in a container, label and freeze. To cook: thaw meat and rice overnight in the refrigerator. Put the rice into the cavity in the shoulder, then put the meat back into shape and secure with string or skewers. Place the meat in a roasting tin and sprinkle it with marjoram, add the dripping and roast until the meat is tender (about 1½ to 2 hours in a moderate oven – 180°C, 350°F, Gas Mark 4). Remove and place on a serving dish. Pour off all but 1 × 15 ml spoon/1 tablespoon of the dripping and stir in the flour, cook, stirring, for 1 minute over a low heat. Add the stock and tomato purée and bring to the boil, add the seasoning and taste and adjust, simmer for 2 minutes then serve with the meat. Garnish with a few sprigs of watercress.
Serves 8

Kidneys in sherry sauce

Metric	Imperial
50 g butter	2 oz butter
1 onion, peeled and chopped	1 onion, peeled and chopped
8 lambs' kidneys	8 lambs' kidneys
50 g button mushrooms, cleaned	2 oz button mushrooms, cleaned
3 × 15 ml spoons flour	3 tablespoons flour
300 ml stock	½ pint stock
6 × 15 ml spoons sherry	6 tablespoons sherry
1 × 15 ml spoon redcurrant jelly	1 tablespoon redcurrant jelly
½ teaspoon salt	½ teaspoon salt
Freshly ground black pepper	Freshly ground black pepper

Cooking Time: 15 minutes

Melt the butter and fry the onion until golden brown. Wash, skin and core the kidneys and cut each into 3 pieces. Add to the pan with the mushrooms and fry for 5 minutes, stirring. Add the flour, stir in the stock, sherry and red-currant jelly with the seasoning, bring to the boil and simmer for 5 minutes.

To freeze: turn into a rigid container, cool, cover, label and freeze.

To serve: place in a casserole and reheat in a moderate oven (180°C, 350°F, Gas Mark 4) for 40 minutes, or until piping hot.

Shoulder of lamb with raisin and apricot stuffing

Metric	Imperial
1 onion, peeled and chopped	1 onion, peeled and chopped
15 g butter	½ oz butter
219 g can apricots	7¾ oz can apricots
50 g fresh white breadcrumbs	2 oz fresh white breadcrumbs
2 × 15 ml spoons finely chopped parsley	2 tablespoons finely chopped parsley
50 g raisins	2 oz raisins
½ teaspoon salt	½ teaspoon salt
Freshly ground black pepper	Freshly ground black pepper
1 egg, beaten	1 egg, beaten
Small boned shoulder of lamb	Small boned shoulder of lamb
Dripping	Dripping

Fry the onion in the butter in a small pan until golden brown. Drain the apricots (reserve the juice to use in the gravy) and roughly chop. Mix the onion with the apricots, breadcrumbs, parsley, raisins and seasoning and bind together with the beaten egg.

To freeze: put the stuffing into the cavity in the meat and sew up or secure with skewers. Place the meat in a polythene bag, seal, label and freeze.

To serve: thaw meat and stuffing overnight in the re-frigerator. Put in a roasting tin with the dripping and roast in a moderate oven (180°C, 350°F, Gas Mark 4) for 1½ to 2 hours, or until tender. Serve with gravy.

Use this recipe within one month.

Braised ox heart

Metric	Imperial
40 g dripping	1½ oz dripping
450 g ox heart, washed, trimmed and sliced	1 lb ox heart, washed, trimmed and sliced
25 g flour	1 oz flour
600 ml water	1 pint water
1 beef stock cube	1 beef stock cube
2 onions, peeled and chopped	2 onions, peeled and chopped
2 carrots, peeled and chopped	2 carrots, peeled and chopped
2 sticks celery, scrubbed and chopped	2 sticks celery, scrubbed and chopped
Salt and freshly ground black pepper	Salt and freshly ground black pepper
1 bay leaf	1 bay leaf
A little gravy browning	A little gravy browning

Cooking Time: 2–3 hours

Heat the dripping in a large pan and fry the ox heart quickly on both sides to brown, remove from the pan. Stir the flour into the fat remaining in the pan and cook for 1 minute, then stir in the water and bring to the boil, add the stock cube and stir until dissolved. Return the heart to the pan with the vegetables, seasoning, bay leaf and gravy brown-ing, cover and simmer until tender (up to 3 hours). Taste and adjust seasoning and remove the bay leaf.

To freeze: turn into a rigid container, cool, cover, label and freeze.

To serve: thaw overnight in the refrigerator. Reheat, preferably in a non-stick pan, for about 10 minutes.

Kidneys in sherry sauce; Pork and corn pies; Braised ox heart; Shoulder of lamb with raisin and apricot stuffing

Pork and corn pies

Metric

350 g lean pork
40 g seasoned flour
25 g dripping
1 large onion, peeled and
finely chopped
300 ml chicken stock
Salt and freshly ground
black pepper
175 g sweetcorn

For the pastry:
350 g plain flour
75 g lard
75 g margarine
Cold water to mix
Milk to glaze

Imperial

12 oz lean pork
1½ oz seasoned flour
1 oz dripping
1 large onion, peeled and
finely chopped
½ pint chicken stock
Salt and freshly ground
black pepper
6 oz sweetcorn

For the pastry:
12 oz plain flour
3 oz lard
3 oz margarine
Cold water to mix
Milk to glaze

Cooking Time: 1½ hours

Trim the pork and cut into ½ in cubes. Toss in the flour. Heat the dripping in a pan, add the onion and fry for 2 to 3 minutes. Add the meat and fry until browned. Stir in the stock and seasoning and bring to the boil, partially cover and simmer for 1¼ hours or until tender, stir in the corn and cook for 2 minutes. Taste and adjust seasoning, leave to become quite cold. Make the pastry in the usual way (see page 48).

Roll out two-thirds of the pastry, cut out three ovals to line three small plates. Roll out the remaining pastry and cut out three ovals for lids. Divide the filling between the pies. Dampen the edges with water and cover with the lids. Seal the edges firmly. Roll out any trimmings and use to decorate the pies.

To freeze: wrap each pie in a double layer of foil, label and freeze.

To serve: unwrap, thaw overnight in the refrigerator or for 4 to 5 hours at room temperature. Make a slit in the centre of each pie, glaze with milk and bake in a hot oven (220°C, 425°F, Gas Mark 7) for 40 minutes, or until the pastry is golden brown.

Makes 3 two-portion pies.

Coq au vin

Coq au vin

Metric	Imperial
25 g butter	1 oz butter
1 × 15 ml spoon oil	1 tablespoon oil
4 chicken joints	4 chicken joints
100 g lean bacon in one piece	4 oz lean bacon in one piece
1 large onion, peeled and sliced	1 large onion, peeled and sliced
2 sticks celery, scrubbed and chopped	2 sticks celery, scrubbed and chopped
1 clove garlic, crushed	1 clove garlic, crushed
25 g flour	1 oz flour
300 ml red wine	½ pint red wine
300 ml stock	½ pint stock
Salt and freshly ground black pepper	Salt and freshly ground black pepper
100 g mushrooms, cleaned	4 oz mushrooms, cleaned

Cooking Time: 1¼ hours

Melt the butter in a pan with the oil. Fry the chicken joints until brown, remove and put in a flameproof casserole. Trim rind from bacon, cut in strips, add to the pan with the onion and celery and fry until soft. Transfer to the casserole. Add the garlic and flour to the fat remaining in the pan and cook until brown. Stir in the wine and stock and bring to the boil, season to taste, pour over the chicken, cover and cook for 45 minutes. Add the mushrooms to the casserole and cook for a further 15 minutes or until the chicken is tender. Taste and adjust seasoning.

To freeze: turn into a rigid container, cool, cover, label and freeze.

To serve: thaw overnight in the refrigerator, turn into a casserole, cover and reheat in a moderate oven (180°C, 350°F, Gas Mark 4) for 45–50 minutes. If liked, put into a heated serving dish.

Country pheasant casserole

Country pheasant casserole

Metric	Imperial
2 × 15 ml spoons oil	2 tablespoons oil
25 g butter	1 oz butter
2 stewing pheasants	2 stewing pheasants
1.5 cm slice streaky	$\frac{1}{2}$ inch slice streaky
bacon, derinded and diced	bacon, derinded and diced
40 g flour	$1\frac{1}{2}$ oz flour
300 ml red wine	$\frac{1}{2}$ pint red wine
300 ml chicken stock	$\frac{1}{2}$ pint chicken stock
2 × 15 ml spoons bramble	2 tablespoons bramble
or apple jelly	or apple jelly
1 × 15 ml spoon	1 tablespoon
Worcestershire sauce	Worcestershire sauce
$\frac{1}{4}$ teaspoon fresh thyme	$\frac{1}{4}$ teaspoon fresh thyme
1 × 5 ml spoon salt	1 teaspoon salt
Plenty of freshly ground	Plenty of freshly ground
black pepper	black pepper
Little gravy browning	Little gravy browning
16 button onions, peeled	16 button onions, peeled

Cooking Time: $2\frac{1}{4}$ hours

Note: stewing birds are cheaper than young birds. Cooked with care they can be even more flavoursome. Mix various birds in the same casserole dish. A pheasant, for instance, can be combined with a brace of pigeons.

Heat oil and butter in a large shallow pan, brown the pheasants over a medium heat, turning as each side becomes golden brown. Lift out on to a plate. Quickly fry the bacon, to extract the fat, in the butter remaining in the pan, lift out and place with the pheasant. Add flour to the pan and cook until a pale golden brown. Slowly add the wine and stock, bring to the boil and allow to thicken. Add the remaining ingredients, except the onions, return the pheasants to the pan, bring to the boil, cover and simmer for $1\frac{1}{2}$ hours, add the onions and cook for a further $\frac{1}{2}$ hour. Test birds for tenderness by piercing the leg with a fine skewer, do not overcook. Lift out the pheasants carefully and carve the meat. Taste and adjust seasoning and, if necessary, add more gravy browning to give a good colour.

To freeze: cool quickly, arrange the slices of pheasant in a rigid container and spoon over the sauce. Cover, label and freeze.

To serve: thaw overnight in the refrigerator, carefully place in a casserole, making sure that the slices of meat are in the bottom of the dish, and reheat in a moderate oven (180°C, 350°F, Gas Mark 4). Arrange the pheasant slices in a heated serving dish and pour over the sauce, put the onions into the dish. Garnish with a sprig of parsley.

Chicken risotto

Metric	Imperial
141 g Savoury Tomato Rice	5 oz Savoury Tomato Rice
225 g cooked chopped chicken	8 oz cooked chopped chicken
100 g cooked chopped frankfurter sausage	4 oz cooked chopped frankfurter sausage

Cook the rice as directed on the packet, remove from the heat and stir in the chicken and frankfurter, mix well. Allow to cool.

To freeze: Place in a rigid container, cover, label and freeze.

To serve: thaw overnight in the refrigerator. Stir in 100 g (4 oz) frozen peas, turn into a well buttered ovenproof dish, cover and heat through in a moderate oven (180°C, 350°F, Gas Mark 4) for 45 minutes.

Chicken paprika

Metric	Imperial
1½ kg chicken	3¼ lb chicken
300 ml dry cider	½ pint dry cider
Salt and freshly ground black pepper	Salt and freshly ground black pepper
25 g butter	1 oz butter
1 onion, peeled and chopped	1 onion, peeled and chopped
3 × 5 ml spoons paprika	3 teaspoons paprika
25 g flour	1 oz flour
450 g tomatoes, skinned and deseeded	1 lb tomatoes, skinned and deseeded
1 clove garlic	1 clove garlic
1 bay leaf	1 bay leaf

Cooking Time: about 2 hours
Oven: 180°C, 350°F, Gas Mark 4

Put the chicken with the giblets in a small roasting tin or casserole, add the cider and seasoning, cover with a piece of foil or a lid and cook in a moderate oven for 1½ hours, or until tender. Lift the chicken out to cool, strain off the stock in the tin and skim off the fat.

Melt the butter in a small pan, add the onion and cook for 5 minutes until soft, stir in the paprika and cook for 3 minutes. Add the flour and stir in the chicken stock with the tomatoes, garlic and bay leaf, simmer without a lid for 15 minutes, remove the bay leaf and taste and adjust the seasoning.

To freeze: carve the chicken into portions, lay in a rigid container and spoon over the sauce (if liked the sauce may be sieved). Cool, cover, label and freeze.

To serve: thaw overnight in the refrigerator, turn into an ovenproof dish, cover and reheat in a moderate oven (180°C, 350°F, Gas Mark 4) for ¾ to 1 hour. Stir in a little soured cream or yogurt just before serving.

Norfolk turkey casserole

Metric	Imperial
4 fresh turkey drum sticks	4 fresh turkey drum sticks
50 g butter	2 oz butter
900 ml packet mushroom soup mix	1½ pint packet mushroom soup mix
450 ml water	¾ pint water
100 g fresh mushrooms, cleaned and sliced	4 oz fresh mushrooms, cleaned and sliced
¼ teaspoon dried thyme	¼ teaspoon dried thyme

Cooking Time: 55 minutes
Oven: 180°C, 350°F, Gas Mark 4

Remove the skin from the drum sticks. Melt the butter in a pan and fry the turkey until golden brown, remove and place in a casserole. Stir the soup mix into the butter remaining in the pan, add the water and bring to the boil, stirring, add the mushrooms and thyme and pour over the drum sticks, cover and cook in a moderate oven for 45 minutes or until tender.

To freeze: cool quickly, turn into a rigid container, cover, label and freeze.

To serve: thaw overnight in the refrigerator, turn into a casserole and reheat in a moderate oven (180°C, 350°F, Gas Mark 4) for 40 minutes.

Chicken risotto; Norfolk turkey casserole; Chicken paprika; Italian country chicken

Italian country chicken

Metric

25 g butter
4 chicken portions
100 g piece smoked
streaky bacon, diced
1 onion, peeled and
chopped
1 clove garlic, crushed
25 g flour
150 ml red Italian wine
150 ml chicken stock
Salt and freshly ground
black pepper
$\frac{1}{4}$ teaspoon dried thyme

Imperial

1 oz butter
4 chicken portions
4 oz piece smoked
streaky bacon, diced
1 onion, peeled and
chopped
1 clove garlic, crushed
1 oz flour
$\frac{1}{4}$ pint red Italian wine
$\frac{1}{4}$ pint chicken stock
Salt and freshly ground
black pepper
$\frac{1}{4}$ teaspoon dried thyme

Cooking Time: $1\frac{1}{4}$ hours
Oven: 160°C, 325°F, Gas Mark 3

Melt the butter in a pan and fry the chicken until brown. Remove and place in a large casserole. Add the bacon to the fat remaining in the pan with the onion and garlic and fry until it is brown and the onion is soft. Stir in the flour and cook for 2 minutes. Add the wine, stock, seasoning and thyme. Bring to the boil and pour over the chicken joints. Cover and cook in a warm oven for 1 hour, or until the chicken is tender. Taste and adjust seasoning. Cool.

To freeze: turn into a rigid container, cover, label and freeze.

To serve: thaw overnight in the refrigerator, turn into a casserole, cover and reheat in a moderate oven (180°C, 350°F, Gas Mark 4) for 45 to 50 minutes.

Chicken in cider sauce with mushrooms

Metric	Imperial
1½ kg chicken	3¼ lb chicken
300 ml dry cider	½ pint dry cider
2 onions, peeled and chopped	2 onions, peeled and chopped
Salt and freshly ground black pepper	Salt and freshly ground black pepper
Milk	Milk
50 g butter	2 oz butter
50 g flour	2 oz flour
175 g mushrooms, cleaned and quartered	6 oz mushrooms, cleaned and quartered

Cooking Time: 1 hour 40 minutes
Oven: 180°C, 350°F, Gas Mark 4

Put the chicken and giblets in a small roasting tin or casserole. Add the cider, onion and seasoning. Cover with a piece of foil or a lid and cook in a moderate oven for 1½ hours or until tender. Lift the chicken out to cool and strain off the remaining stock in the tin, skim off the fat and make up to 750 ml (1¼ pints) with milk. Remove the chicken meat from the carcass, and cut it into good sized pieces. Melt the butter in a pan, add the flour, cook and stir in the stock and milk, bring to the boil, stirring, and allow to thicken. Add the mushrooms and cook for 5 minutes. Taste and adjust seasoning, stir in the chicken, turn into a rigid container and leave to cool.

To freeze: cover, label and freeze.

To serve: thaw overnight in the refrigerator, turn into a casserole and put in a moderate oven (180°C, 350°F, Gas Mark 4) for 45 minutes or until piping hot, turn into a heated serving dish.

Chicken in cider sauce with mushrooms

Calpe chicken

Metric	Imperial
100 g prunes	4 oz prunes
50 g butter	2 oz butter
4 chicken portions	4 chicken portions
4 rashers streaky bacon, chopped	4 rashers streaky bacon, chopped
1 onion, peeled and chopped	1 onion, peeled and chopped
1 carrot, peeled and sliced	1 carrot, peeled and sliced
3 sticks celery, scrubbed and sliced	3 sticks celery, scrubbed and sliced
40 g flour	1½ oz flour
150 ml red wine	¼ pint red wine
450 ml chicken stock	¾ pint chicken stock
Finely grated rind of ½ lemon	Finely grated rind of ½ lemon
Salt and freshly ground black pepper	Salt and freshly ground black pepper

Cooking Time: 1¼ hours
Oven: 180°C, 350°F, Gas Mark 4

Soak the prunes overnight and then remove the stones. Melt the butter in a pan and brown the chicken on both sides, remove and place in a casserole. Add the bacon, onion, carrot and celery to the pan and fry for 3 to 4 minutes. Stir in the flour and cook for a minute. Add the remaining ingredients and bring to the boil, simmer for 1 minute to allow to thicken. Pour over the chicken, cover the casserole and cook in a moderate oven for about 1 hour or until the chicken is tender.

To freeze: turn into a rigid container, cool, cover, label and freeze.

To serve: thaw overnight in the refrigerator, or for 5 to 6 hours at room temperature, place in a casserole and reheat in a moderately hot oven (190°C, 375°F, Gas Mark 5) for ¾ to 1 hour.

Calpe chicken

Chicken with olives

Metric	Imperial
25 g butter	1 oz butter
4 chicken joints	4 chicken joints
100 g piece streaky bacon, cut in one thick slice	4 oz piece streaky bacon, cut in one thick slice
12 button onions, peeled	12 button onions, peeled
25 g flour	1 oz flour
150 ml dry cider	¼ pint dry cider
150 ml water or chicken stock	¼ pint water or chicken stock
Salt and freshly ground black pepper	Salt and freshly ground black pepper

Cooking Time: 1¼ hours
Oven: 180°C, 350°F, Gas Mark 4

Melt the butter in a frying pan and fry the chicken until golden brown all over, remove and place in a casserole. Cut the bacon in strips, add to the frying pan with the onions and fry until brown, transfer to the casserole. Stir the flour into the butter remaining in the pan and cook for 2 minutes, add the cider and water or stock and bring to the boil, stirring, season to taste, pour over the chicken and cook in a moderate oven for 1 hour, or until tender.

To freeze: cool, turn into a large foil dish or rigid container, cover, label and freeze.

To serve: thaw overnight in the refrigerator, turn into a casserole and reheat in a moderately hot oven (190°C, 375°F, Gas Mark 5) for 45 minutes. Stir in 12 stuffed green olives, taste, adjust seasoning. If liked, put on to a heated dish and garnish with chopped parsley and croûtons.

Simple Devon chicken pie; Braised pigeons

Chicken with olives

Simple Devon chicken pie

Metric	Imperial
225 g cooked chicken	8 oz cooked chicken
225 g cooked bacon or ham	8 oz cooked bacon or ham
100 g frozen mixed vegetables, blanched	4 oz frozen mixed vegetables, blanched
298 g can condensed mushroom soup	10½ oz can condensed mushroom soup
212 g packet shortcrust pastry	7½ oz packet shortcrust pastry

Cut the chicken and ham into small even-sized pieces and place in a bowl with the vegetables and soup, mix well together. Turn into a 1 l (1½ pint) pie dish. Roll out the pastry and use to cover the top of the pie, cut any trimmings into leaves and use as decoration.

To freeze: open freeze to prevent the decoration from being crushed. Put into a polythene bag, seal, label and freeze.

To cook: remove from the bag, thaw overnight in the refrigerator, brush the top with milk and make two small slits in the centre. Bake in a moderately hot oven (200°C, 400°F, Gas Mark 6) for about 30 minutes or until the pastry is golden brown.

Braised pigeons

Metric	Imperial
2 pigeons, split	2 pigeons, split
50 g dripping	2 oz dripping
225 g onions, peeled and sliced	8 oz onions, peeled and sliced
40 g flour	1½ oz flour
600 ml stock	1 pint stock
3 × 15 ml spoons tomato ketchup	3 tablespoons tomato ketchup
½ teaspoon fresh or dried marjoram	½ teaspoon fresh or dried marjoram
A few drops Worcestershire sauce	A few drops Worcestershire sauce
Salt and freshly ground black pepper	Salt and freshly ground black pepper

Cooking Time: 50 minutes to 1 hour

Wipe the pigeons. Melt the dripping in a large pan, add the pigeons and fry quickly to brown, remove and put on one side, add the onion and fry for 5 to 10 minutes until golden brown. Stir in the flour and cook for 2 minutes, add the stock and bring to the boil, stirring until thickened, add the remaining ingredients and return pigeons to the pan, cover and simmer gently for 40 to 50 minutes, or until tender – the time will depend on the age of the birds.

To freeze: turn into a rigid container, cool, cover, label and freeze.

To serve: thaw overnight in the refrigerator, place in a casserole, cover and reheat in a moderate oven (180°C, 350°F, Gas Mark 4) for ¾ to 1 hour. Serve with red cabbage (see page 48).

43

Smoked haddock pancake rolls

Metric	Imperial
212 g buttered smoked haddock fillets	7½ oz buttered smoked haddock fillets
Milk	Milk
25 g margarine	1 oz margarine
25 g flour	1 oz flour
Finely grated rind of ½ lemon	Finely grated rind of ½ lemon
Freshly ground black pepper	Freshly ground black pepper
8 pancakes (see page 55)	8 pancakes (see page 55)

Cooking Time: about 15 minutes

Cook the haddock as directed on the packet, drain off the liquor and make up to 300 ml (½ pint) with milk. Skin and flake the fish and remove any bones. Melt the margarine in a small pan and add the flour, cook for one minute, stir in the fish liquor, bring to boil, simmer for 2 minutes to thicken. Add the haddock, lemon rind and pepper, taste and adjust seasoning. Divide the filling between the pancakes, fold in the sides and roll up.

To freeze: wrap in a double layer of foil, seal, label and freeze.

To serve: unwrap, thaw at room temperature for 4 to 5 hours. Melt 50–75 g (2–3 oz) butter in a frying pan and fry the pancake rolls over a moderate heat until golden brown all over and hot through. Serve with a green vegetable.

Salmon fish cakes; Family fish pie

Smoked haddock pancake rolls

Salmon fish cakes

Metric	Imperial
226 g can pink salmon	8 oz can pink salmon
350 g freshly boiled sieved potatoes	12 oz freshly boiled sieved potatoes
1 × 15 ml spoon finely chopped parsley	1 tablespoon finely chopped parsley
Salt and freshly ground black pepper	Salt and freshly ground black pepper
2 eggs, beaten	2 eggs, beaten
Brown crumbs	Brown crumbs

Drain the salmon, flake the fish and remove any black skin and bones.

Place in a bowl with the potato, parsley, seasoning and one beaten egg. Mix well and shape into a roll, cut into 8 even-sized slices. Coat the fish cakes in the other beaten egg and then toss them in the brown crumbs.

To freeze: open freeze, then pack in a rigid container, cover, label and return to the freezer.

To cook and serve: thaw at room temperature for 3 to 4 hours, then fry in hot oil for 4 to 5 minutes on each side until golden brown, drain on kitchen paper. Serve with a mixed salad.

Family fish pie

Metric	Imperial
450 g cod	1 lb cod
225 g shelled peas	8 oz shelled peas
450 ml milk	$\frac{3}{4}$ pint milk
40 g butter	$1\frac{1}{2}$ oz butter
40 g flour	$1\frac{1}{2}$ oz flour
3 hard-boiled eggs	3 hard-boiled eggs
2 × 15 ml spoons mayonnaise	2 tablespoons mayonnaise
Salt and freshly ground black pepper	Salt and freshly ground black pepper
675 g potatoes, peeled	$1\frac{1}{2}$ lb potatoes, peeled
Milk and butter	Milk and butter

Cooking Time: about 12 minutes

Skin and wash the cod, put in a pan with the peas and milk and simmer gently for 10 minutes, or until the fish can be flaked with a fork. Tip into a bowl and set on one side. Rinse out the pan and then melt the butter. Remove from the heat and stir in the flour, add the milk strained from the fish, return to the heat and bring to the boil. Remove any bones from the fish and add to the sauce with the peas, chopped hard-boiled eggs, mayonnaise and seasoning. Turn into a $1\frac{3}{4}$ l (3 pint) foil dish, leave to cool.

Boil the potatoes, drain, mash with milk and butter, taste and adjust seasoning. Spread or pipe a border round the edge of the dish.

To freeze: cool, cover, label and freeze.

To serve: thaw overnight in the refrigerator, then remove lid and reheat in a hot oven (220°C, 425°F, Gas Mark 7) for 30 to 40 minutes. Garnish with sprigs of parsley and sliced tomato.

Pizza

Metric	Imperial
850 g packet white bread mix	*1 lb 14 oz packet white bread mix*
A little oil	*A little oil*

A yeast dough takes time to make, but the new bread mixes are quick and easy to use, can be made in a quarter of the time and offer an ideal base for delicious toppings.

It is a good idea to make at least two pizzas at one go – more if you can. If you like the toppings, but find the bases a bit much of a good thing, simply make them thinner.

Pizzas are usually round, but if every inch of your freezer space is valuable, oblong pizzas can be stacked into block shapes, which take up less room. Make them in a small Swiss roll tin and cut to the size you want. Of course, there is no rule about size – make one big family pizza, or a lot of individual-sized ones. Experiment and find what suits you best. Do the same with flavours – you can always add to these by sprinkling at the last minute with a generous amount of grated cheese, or a few chopped herbs.

Make up the complete bread mix as directed on the packet, knead lightly until smooth then divide into 4 equal portions. Roll each piece out into a circle 20 cm (8 in) in diameter and brush each with oil.

Topping 1:

Metric	Imperial
3 slices salami	*3 slices salami*
4 × 15 ml spoons tomato chutney	*4 tablespoons tomato chutney*
¼ teaspoon mixed herbs	*¼ teaspoon mixed herbs*
2 large tomatoes, sliced	*2 large tomatoes, sliced*

Topping 1:
Arrange the slices of salami on a dough circle, put the chutney and herbs in a bowl and mix well, spread over the salami. Arrange the tomato slices on the chutney to cover completely.

Topping 4:

Metric	Imperial
85 g can chicken and bacon spread	*3 oz can chicken and bacon spread*
226 g can peeled tomatoes, drained and roughly chopped	*8 oz can peeled tomatoes, drained and roughly chopped*
1 × 15 ml spoon oil	*1 tablespoon oil*
1 onion, peeled and chopped	*1 onion, peeled and chopped*
Freshly ground black pepper	*Freshly ground black pepper*
6 stuffed green olives, sliced	*6 stuffed green olives, sliced*

Topping 4:
Spread a dough circle with the chicken and bacon spread. Place the onion and oil in a pan and cook for 5 minutes, stir in the tomatoes with the pepper and olives, mix well, cool and spread on the dough.

Topping 2:

Metric	Imperial
396 g can tomatoes, drained and roughly chopped	*14 oz can tomatoes, drained and roughly chopped*
¼ teaspoon oregano	*¼ teaspoon oregano*
Salt and freshly ground black pepper	*Salt and freshly ground black pepper*
75 g Emmenthal cheese	*3 oz Emmenthal cheese*
Anchovy fillets	*Anchovy fillets*

Topping 2:
Mix the tomatoes with the oregano and seasoning, spread over the dough. Cover with slices of cheese and arrange a lattice of anchovy fillets on top.

Topping 3:

Metric	Imperial
25 g butter	*1 oz butter*
4 rashers streaky bacon, chopped	*4 rashers streaky bacon, chopped*
50 g button mushrooms, cleaned and sliced	*2 oz button mushrooms, cleaned and sliced*
50 g Cheddar cheese, grated	*2 oz Cheddar cheese, grated*

Topping 3:
Melt the butter in a small pan, add the bacon and mushrooms and cook together for 5 minutes, drain and arrange on the dough, cover with grated cheese.

Leave all the pizzas to prove in a warm place for 30 minutes. To freeze: open freeze until firm, then wrap in a double thickness of foil, label and return to the freezer.
To cook: unwrap, place on a lightly oiled baking tray and bake in oven (220°C, 425°F, Gas Mark 7) 25–30 minutes.

Pizzas: Topping 1; Topping 2; Topping 3; Topping 4

Red cabbage

Metric	Imperial
1 small red cabbage	1 small red cabbage
350 g cooking apples, peeled, cored and sliced	12 oz cooking apples, peeled, cored and sliced
150 ml water	1/4 pint water
40 g sugar	1 1/2 oz sugar
1 × 5 ml spoon salt	1 teaspoon salt
3 cloves	3 cloves
5 × 15 ml spoons vinegar	5 tablespoons vinegar
50 g butter	2 oz butter
1 × 15 ml spoon redcurrant jelly	1 tablespoon redcurrant jelly

Cooking Time: 45 minutes

Finely shred the cabbage, removing the hard stalk, and place with the apples and water in a pan. Add sugar, salt and cloves, cover and simmer until tender, about 45 minutes. Remove the cloves, add the vinegar, butter and redcurrant jelly and stir until the butter has melted. Taste and adjust seasoning.

To freeze: turn into a rigid container, cool, cover, label and freeze.

To serve: thaw overnight in the refrigerator, put in a non-stick pan and reheat gently, stirring.

Leek and ham flan

Metric	Imperial
For the pastry:	For the pastry:
100 g plain flour	4 oz plain flour
25 g margarine	1 oz margarine
25 g lard	1 oz lard
1 × 15 ml spoon cold water	1 tablespoon cold water
For the filling:	For the filling:
25 g butter	1 oz butter
1 leek, washed and finely sliced	1 leek, washed and finely sliced
100 g cooked ham, chopped	4 oz cooked ham, chopped
Salt and freshly ground black pepper	Salt and freshly ground black pepper
1 egg	1 egg
150 ml single cream	1/4 pint single cream

Cooking Time: 40–45 minutes
Oven: 220°C, 425°F, Gas Mark 7
180°C, 350°F, Gas Mark 4

Sieve the flour into a bowl, add the fats cut in small pieces and rub in with the fingertips until the mixture resembles fine breadcrumbs, add water and mix to a firm dough. Roll out and line an 18 cm (7 in) plain flan ring on a baking sheet. Chill in the refrigerator for 10 minutes. Fill with greaseproof paper and baking beans and bake blind in a hot oven for 15 minutes. Remove from oven and take out the beans and paper. Meanwhile melt the butter in a small pan, add the leek and cook slowly until soft but not brown, then drain and put in the flan case with the ham. Blend the seasoning, egg and cream together and pour into the flan. Reduce the oven temperature and bake the flan for 25 to 30 minutes or until the filling is set.

To freeze: cool, put in a polythene bag, seal, label and freeze.

To serve: remove from bag and thaw in the refrigerator overnight, then heat through in a moderate oven (180°C, 350°F, Gas Mark 4) for 25 minutes.

Onion and anchovy flan

Metric	Imperial
450 g onions, peeled and finely sliced	1 lb onions, peeled and finely sliced
25 g butter	1 oz butter
2 × 15 ml spoons oil	2 tablespoons oil
1 clove garlic, crushed	1 clove garlic, crushed
Pastry made with 100 g flour (see above)	Pastry made with 4 oz flour (see above)
1 large egg	1 large egg
4 × 15 ml spoons double cream	4 tablespoons double cream
Salt and freshly ground black pepper	Salt and freshly ground black pepper
70 g can anchovies	2 1/2 oz can anchovies

Cooking Time: about 1 1/2 hours
Oven: 200°C, 400°F, Gas Mark 6

Put the onion in a pan with the butter, oil and garlic, cover and cook very slowly with the lid on until soft and golden, this may take up to one hour. Make the pastry, roll out, line an 18 cm (7 in) flan ring on a baking sheet and leave to rest. Remove the onion from the heat and leave to cool slightly. Beat the egg with the cream and seasoning, stir into the onion and put into the flan case. Arrange a lattice of anchovy fillets on top of the flan and bake in a moderately hot oven for about 30 minutes or until set.

To freeze: cool, put in a polythene bag, seal, label and freeze.

To serve: thaw in the refrigerator for several hours, then heat in a moderate oven (180°C, 350°F, Gas Mark 4) for 25 minutes.

Red cabbage; Stuffed aubergines; Onion and anchovy flan; Leek and ham flan

Stuffed aubergines

Metric	Imperial
2 onions, peeled and chopped	*2 onions, peeled and chopped*
1 clove garlic, crushed (optional)	*1 clove garlic, crushed (optional)*
350 g minced beef	*12 oz minced beef*
40 g flour	*1½ oz flour*
300 ml water	*½ pint water*
1 × 5 ml spoon Worcestershire sauce	*1 teaspoon Worcestershire sauce*
1 beef stock cube	*1 beef stock cube*
Salt and freshly ground black pepper	*Salt and freshly ground black pepper*
2 large aubergines	*2 large aubergines*
300 ml cheese sauce (see page 29)	*½ pint cheese sauce (see page 29)*

Cooking Time: 35 minutes

Put the onion and garlic with the mince in a pan and fry gently for 5 minutes, stirring frequently. Stir in the flour and water, Worcestershire sauce and add the crumbled stock cube and seasoning. Cover and simmer slowly for 30 minutes or until tender, taste and adjust seasoning. Cool. Halve the aubergines lengthwise and scoop out the centres. Cook the shells in boiling water for 5 minutes, drain well and place in a large foil dish. Fill with the beef mixture (to which the coarsely chopped aubergine flesh can be added if liked) and spoon over the cheese sauce.

To freeze: leave to become quite cold, cover, label and freeze.

To serve: thaw at room temperature for 6 hours, then cook in a moderate oven (180°C, 350°F, Gas Mark 4) for 40 minutes or until hot through.

49

Cabbage and onion sauté

Metric	Imperial
1 kg hard white cabbage	2 lb hard white cabbage
1–2 × 5 ml spoons salt	1–2 teaspoons salt
50 g butter	2 oz butter
1 onion, peeled and chopped	1 onion, peeled and chopped
Freshly ground black pepper	Freshly ground black pepper

Cooking Time: about 7 minutes

Shred the cabbage fairly finely and remove all the hard white stalk, sprinkle with salt and leave to stand for 10 minutes in a bowl of cold water. Drain off the water, but do not rinse off the salt. Melt 25 g (1 oz) butter in a large saucepan, add the cabbage and cook until just tender, but still crisp, shaking the pan frequently to prevent sticking. Turn into a bowl. Melt the remaining butter in the pan and fry the onion until golden brown, stir into the cabbage and season with plenty of pepper. Cool.

To freeze: turn into a rigid container, cover, label and freeze.

To serve: thaw at room temperature for 5 to 6 hours, turn into a saucepan and reheat gently, stirring continuously.

Spinach and cheese flan

Metric	Imperial
For the pastry:	For the pastry:
175 g plain flour	6 oz plain flour
40 g margarine	1½ oz margarine
40 g lard	1½ oz lard
Water to mix	Water to mix
For the filling:	For the filling:
226 g packet chopped spinach	8 oz packet chopped spinach
1 egg	1 egg
150 ml single cream	¼ pint single cream
Salt and freshly ground black pepper	Salt and freshly ground black pepper
75 g grated Cheddar cheese	3 oz grated Cheddar cheese

Cooking Time: 40–45 minutes
Oven: 220°C, 425°F, Gas Mark 7
180°C, 350°F, Gas Mark 4

Sieve the flour into a bowl, rub in the margarine and lard until the mixture resembles fine breadcrumbs, add sufficient cold water to make a firm dough. Roll out and line a 20 cm (8 in) plain flan ring on a baking sheet. Chill in the refrigerator for 10 minutes. Fill with greaseproof paper and baking beans and bake blind in a hot oven for 15 minutes.

Remove from oven, take out beans and paper. Cook the spinach as directed on the packet, drain very thoroughly and spread over the bottom of the flan. Blend the egg, cream and seasonings together and pour into the flan case. Sprinkle with the cheese. Reduce the oven temperature and bake the flan for about 30 minutes or until the filling is set.

To freeze: cool, put in a polythene bag, seal, freeze.

To serve: thaw in the refrigerator overnight, then heat through in a moderate oven (180°C, 350°F, Gas Mark 4) for 25 minutes.

Asparagus flan

Metric	Imperial
Pastry made with 100 g plain flour (see page 48)	Pastry made with 4 oz plain flour (see page 48)
298 g can green cut asparagus tips, drained	10½ oz can green cut asparagus tips, drained
1 egg	1 egg
150 ml single cream	¼ pint single cream
Salt and freshly ground black pepper	Salt and freshly ground black pepper

Cooking Time: about 45 minutes
Oven: 220°C, 425°F, Gas Mark 7
180°C, 350°F, Gas Mark 4

Roll out the pastry and use to line an 18 cm (7 in) flan ring on a baking sheet. Chill in the refrigerator for 10 minutes. Fill with greaseproof paper and baking beans and bake blind for 15 minutes in a hot oven. Remove from the oven and take out the beans and paper. Reserve 10 asparagus tips and put the remainder in the bottom of the flan case. Blend the egg, cream and seasoning together and pour into the flan. Reduce the oven temperature and bake the flan for 15 minutes. Arrange the reserved asparagus tips on top and return to the oven for a further 15 minutes, until the filling is set.

To freeze: cool, put in a polythene bag, seal, label and freeze.

To serve: thaw in the refrigerator overnight, then heat through in a moderate oven (180°C, 350°F, Gas Mark 4) for 25 minutes.

Celery and ham mornay; Cabbage and onion sauté; Asparagus flan; Spinach and cheese flan

Celery and ham mornay

Metric	Imperial
538 g can celery hearts, drained	*1 lb 3 oz can celery hearts, drained*
4 slices ham	*4 slices ham*
300 ml cheese sauce (see page 29)	*½ pint cheese sauce (see page 29)*

Wrap each piece of celery in a slice of ham. Lay in an oven-proof dish, pour over the cheese sauce. Cool.

To freeze: cover with a piece of foil, seal, label and freeze.

To cook: thaw at room temperature for 5 to 6 hours, sprinkle with 50 g (2 oz) grated Cheddar cheese and cook in a moderately hot oven (200°C, 400°F, Gas Mark 6) for 30 minutes or until golden brown.

Lattice mince pie

Metric	Imperial
150 g plain flour	6 oz plain flour
50 g butter	2 oz butter
50 g lard	2 oz lard
Pinch of salt	Pinch of salt
1 egg yolk	1 egg yolk
15 g caster sugar	½ oz caster sugar
2 × 5 ml spoons water	2 teaspoons water
450 g freezer mincemeat	1 lb freezer mincemeat
(see page 91)	(see page 91)
Milk to glaze	Milk to glaze

Cooking Time: 25 minutes
Oven: 200°C, 400°F, Gas Mark 6

Sieve the flour into a bowl, add the fats cut in small pieces, with the pinch of salt, and rub into the flour with the fingertips until the mixture resembles fine breadcrumbs. Mix the egg yolk, sugar and water together, add to the dry ingredients and bind them together. Roll out the pastry and line a 20 cm (8 in) pie plate. Flute the edges. Spread the mincemeat over the pastry. Roll out the pastry trimmings and cut into 6 strips about 1.5 cm (½ in) wide and long enough to go across the top of the pie. Twist each strip once or twice and lay them loosely over the mincemeat, three each way to make a lattice. Damp edges and press firmly to the pastry. Brush the pastry with a little milk and bake in a moderately hot oven for 25 minutes, or until a pale golden brown, cool.

To freeze: cover with a polythene bag, seal, label and freeze.

To serve: thaw at room temperature for 4 hours then reheat in a moderately hot oven (190°C, 375°F, Gas Mark 5) for 20 minutes, or serve cold.

Lattice mince pie; Little mince pies

Little mince pies

Metric	Imperial
450 g self-raising flour	*1 lb self-raising flour*
100 g butter	*4 oz butter*
100 g hard margarine	*4 oz hard margarine*
50 g lard	*2 oz lard*
1 egg, separated	*1 egg, separated*
Milk	*Milk*
675 g freezer mincemeat	*1½ lb freezer mincemeat*
(see page 91)	*(see page 91)*
A little caster sugar	*A little caster sugar*

Cooking Time: 20 minutes
Oven: 200°C, 400°F, Gas Mark 6

Sieve the flour into a bowl. Add the butter, margarine and lard cut in small pieces, then rub the fats into the flour until the mixture resembles fine breadcrumbs. Add the egg yolk with enough milk to make a firm dough. Knead until blended then chill the dough in the refrigerator for 20 minutes. Roll out half the dough thinly. Cut out about 35 circles 7 cm (2¾ in) in diameter and use to line tart tins. Fill with the mincemeat. Roll out the remaining dough and cut out 35 circles 6 cm (2¼ in) in diameter for the lids. Wet the edges of the dough circles in the tin and press the lids on gently to seal. Lightly beat the egg white and brush over the tops of the pies, dust with a little sugar. Bake in a moderately hot oven for 20 minutes, or until the pastry is crisp and golden brown. Leave to cool in the tins.
To freeze: open freeze in the tins, then remove from tins and pack in polythene bags, seal and label.
To serve: replace in the tins and reheat in a moderately hot oven (200°C, 400°F, Gas Mark 6) for 25 minutes.
Makes about 35 mince pies

Fresh mincemeat pancakes; Rich orange pancakes; Apricot and almond flan; Prune and apple pie

Prune and apple pie

Metric

100 g prunes, soaked
675 g cooking apples,
peeled, cored and sliced
100 g soft brown sugar
50 g butter
1 × 5 ml spoon ground
cinnamon
Pastry made with 225 g
flour (see page 48)
Milk to glaze

Imperial

4 oz prunes, soaked
1½ lb cooking apples,
peeled, cored and sliced
4 oz soft brown sugar
2 oz butter
1 teaspoon ground
cinnamon
Pastry made with 8 oz
flour (see page 48)
Milk to glaze

Cooking Time: about 15 minutes

Remove the stones from the prunes. Place the prunes and apples in a pan with the sugar, butter and cinnamon. Cook gently until the apples are just tender, stirring occasionally, leave to cool.

Make up the pastry and use half to line a 20 cm (8 in) ovenproof, enamel or foil plate. Spread in the filling. Moisten the edges with water and roll out the remaining pastry to cover, press edges well together and flute. Use any trimmings to decorate the pie.

To freeze: open freeze, then cover with a lid of foil, label and return to the freezer.

To serve: remove the foil lid, make two small slits in the top, brush with a little milk and bake in a hot oven (220°C, 425°F, Gas Mark 7) for 30 to 40 minutes, or until golden brown. Serve with cream or ice-cream.

Apricot and almond flan

Metric	Imperial
Pastry made with 100 g flour (see page 48)	Pastry made with 4 oz flour (see page 48)
425 g can apricots	15 oz can apricots
150 g flour, sifted	5 oz flour, sifted
25 g ground almonds	1 oz ground almonds
75 g butter	3 oz butter
50 g caster sugar	2 oz caster sugar

Cooking Time: 45 minutes
Oven: 200°C, 400°F, Gas Mark 6
  160°C, 325°F, Gas Mark 3

Roll out the pastry and line an 18 cm (7 in) fluted flan dish. Drain the apricots and arrange half over the base of the flan. Mix the flour with the almonds and rub in the butter, stir in the sugar. Cover the apricots with a layer of this mixture. Place the rest of the apricots on top and cover with the remaining almond mixture, pressing down firmly. Bake in a moderately hot oven for 15 minutes, then reduce the oven temperature and cook for a further 30 minutes, or until a pale golden brown.
To freeze: cool, wrap in foil, label and freeze.
To serve: thaw at room temperature for 5 to 6 hours, mix a pinch of cinnamon with a little caster sugar and sprinkle over the flan, serve with plenty of cream.

Rich orange pancakes

Metric	Imperial
100 g plain flour	4 oz plain flour
¼ teaspoon salt	¼ teaspoon salt
1 egg	1 egg
1 × 15 ml spoon oil	1 tablespoon oil
300 ml milk	½ pint milk
175 g unsalted butter	6 oz unsalted butter
Finely grated rind of one orange	Finely grated rind of one orange
2–3 × 15 ml spoons orange juice	2–3 tablespoons orange juice
225 g sifted icing sugar	8 oz sifted icing sugar

Sieve the flour and salt into a bowl. Blend in the egg with the oil and milk. Heat a very little oil in a 20 cm (8 in) pan. Drop 2 × 15 ml spoons (2 tablespoons) of the mixture into the pan and tilt and rotate to spread out the batter. Cook for 1 minute, then turn over and cook the other side for 1 minute. Turn out and make seven more pancakes.
Cream the butter with the orange rind and beat in as much orange juice as possible and the icing sugar.
Divide the filling between the pancakes and spread over each, then fold in four.
To freeze: wrap in a double thickness of foil, seal, label and freeze.
To cook and serve: thaw at room temperature for 4 hours. Heat a very little butter in a frying pan, add the pancakes and fry gently for 3 to 4 minutes on each side. Turn on to a serving dish and sprinkle with a little icing sugar. Serve at once.

Fresh mincemeat pancakes

Metric	Imperial
450 g cooking apples, peeled, cored and sliced	1 lb cooking apples, peeled, cored and sliced
100 g soft brown sugar	4 oz soft brown sugar
50 g butter	2 oz butter
¼ teaspoon mixed spice	¼ teaspoon mixed spice
175 g mixed dried fruit	6 oz mixed dried fruit
1 × 15 ml spoon lemon juice	1 tablespoon lemon juice
A little finely grated lemon rind	A little finely grated lemon rind
8 pancakes (see above)	8 pancakes (see above)

Cooking Time: 20 minutes

Place the apples in a pan with the sugar, butter and spice and simmer gently, stirring occasionally, for 20 minutes or until tender.
Stir in the dried fruit, lemon juice and rind and leave to cool.
Divide the filling between the pancakes and roll up.
To freeze: wrap in a double thickness of foil, seal, label and freeze.
To cook and serve: unwrap and thaw at room temperature for 4 hours. Fry the pancake rolls in about 75 g (3 oz) butter over a moderate heat until they are golden brown. Serve with plenty of cream.

Orange sorbet

Metric	Imperial
175 g sugar	6 oz sugar
450 ml water	¾ pint water
178 ml can frozen orange juice, thawed	6¼ fl oz can frozen orange juice, thawed
2 egg whites	2 egg whites

Dissolve the sugar in the water, bring to the boil and boil, uncovered, for 10 minutes. Turn the thawed orange juice into a bowl and pour on the syrup. Leave to get cold then pour into a 600 ml (1 pint) ice-cube tray and freeze to a mushy consistency. Whisk the egg whites until thick and foamy but not dry. Fold into the orange mixture and return to the freezer until firm.

To freeze: cover, label and return to freezer.

To serve: leave to soften slightly in the refrigerator for about 5 minutes then serve spooned into glasses.

Raspberry sorbet

Metric	Imperial
450 g raspberries	1 lb raspberries
175 g sugar	6 oz sugar
2 egg whites	2 egg whites

Sieve the raspberries and measure the amount of water needed to make the purée up to 600 ml (1 pint) – do not mix the purée and water together. Dissolve the sugar in the water and bring to the boil, boil uncovered for 10 minutes, stir into the raspberry purée and leave to cool, then pour into a 600 ml (1 pint) ice-cube tray and freeze until it has a mushy consistency. Whisk the egg whites until thick and foamy, but not dry, and fold into the purée, return to the freezer until firm.

To freeze: cover, label and return to freezer.

To serve: leave to soften slightly in the refrigerator for about 5 minutes then spoon into glasses.

Red fruit salad

Metric	Imperial
225 g rhubarb, cut in 2 cm lengths	8 oz rhubarb, cut in ¾ inch lengths
225 g blackcurrants	8 oz blackcurrants
225 g granulated sugar	8 oz granulated sugar
6 × 15 ml spoons water	6 tablespoons water
225 g small strawberries, hulled	8 oz small strawberries, hulled
225 g raspberries	8 oz raspberries

Put the rhubarb in a saucepan with the blackcurrants. Add the sugar and water and bring to the boil, simmering until barely tender, stirring; this will take only a few minutes. Add the strawberries and raspberries and cook for a further minute.

To freeze: turn into a rigid container, cool, cover, label and freeze.

To serve: thaw at room temperature for 8 hours, or overnight in the refrigerator. Stir in a little brandy to taste. Turn into a serving dish and serve with cream.

Blackcurrant sorbet

Metric	Imperial
1 kg blackcurrants	2 lb blackcurrants
175 g caster sugar	6 oz caster sugar
900 ml water	1½ pints water
2 × 15 ml spoons lemon juice	2 tablespoons lemon juice
3 × 15 ml spoons rum	3 tablespoons rum

Cook the blackcurrants with the sugar and water. Add the lemon juice and sieve. Turn into a shallow container and freeze until mushy. Take out and whisk until light and fluffy and add the rum. Return to the freezer and freeze until firm.
To freeze: cover, label and return to freezer.
To serve: leave to soften slightly in the refrigerator for 5 minutes, then serve.

Lemon cream ice

Metric	Imperial
225 g caster sugar	8 oz caster sugar
8 egg yolks	8 egg yolks
4 × 15 ml spoons lemon juice	4 tablespoons lemon juice
300 ml double cream	½ pint double cream

This is a very good way of using up egg yolks if you have been making meringues.
Put the sugar on an enamel plate and heat through in the oven or under the grill. Put the yolks in a large bowl, pour on the hot sugar and whisk at once until thick and light. Put the lemon juice and cream in a bowl and whisk until the cream forms soft peaks, fold into the egg mixture, turn into a 1¼ l (2 pint) rigid polythene container.
To freeze: cover, label and freeze.
To serve: leave to stand at room temperature for 5 minutes then serve – give small portions as the ice-cream is very rich.
Serves 6 to 8

Blackcurrant sorbet; Lemon cream ice

Strawberry ice-cream

Metric	Imperial
225 g strawberries, hulled	8 oz strawberries, hulled
50 g granulated sugar	2 oz granulated sugar
2 eggs	2 eggs
50 g caster sugar	2 oz caster sugar
1 small can evaporated milk, well chilled	1 small can evaporated milk, well chilled

Place the strawberries in a pan with the granulated sugar and cook gently until soft, about 5 minutes. Sieve and leave to become quite cold. Separate the eggs. Place the yolks in a small bowl and blend with a fork; put the whites in a large bowl and whisk until stiff, then whisk in the caster sugar a spoon at a time. Slowly whisk the egg yolks into the whites. Whisk the evaporated milk in a bowl until thick and fold into the egg mixture with the strawberry purée.

Turn into a 900 ml (1½ pint) dish and leave to freeze for at least 4 hours or until set.

To freeze: cover, label and return to freezer.

To serve: leave to stand at room temperature for about 5 minutes then serve.

Note: this is a good way of using frozen strawberries.

Caramel ice-cream

Metric	Imperial
75 g fresh brown breadcrumbs	3 oz fresh brown breadcrumbs
50 g demerara sugar	2 oz demerara sugar
4 eggs, separated	4 eggs, separated
100 g caster sugar	4 oz caster sugar
300 ml double cream	½ pint double cream

Place the breadcrumbs and demerara sugar on an enamel or foil plate and toast under a hot grill until golden brown and caramelised, stirring occasionally. This will take 5 to 8 minutes. Leave to become quite cold.

Whisk the egg yolks in a small bowl until well blended. In another, larger, bowl whisk the egg whites until stiff then whisk in the caster sugar a teaspoon at a time. Whisk the cream until it forms soft peaks, then fold into the meringue mixture with the egg yolks and breadcrumbs. Turn into a 1½ l (2½ pint) rigid container.

To freeze: cover, label and freeze.

To serve: thaw at room temperature for 5 minutes, then serve in spoonfuls with biscuits.

Serves 6 to 8

Strawberry ice-cream; Caramel ice-cream

Redcurrant and raspberry mousse

Metric	Imperial
100 g sugar	4 oz sugar
300 ml water	½ pint water
225 g redcurrants	8 oz redcurrants
225 g raspberries	8 oz raspberries
15 g gelatine	½ oz gelatine
1 × 15 ml spoon cold water	1 tablespoon cold water
3 × 15 ml spoons orange juice	3 tablespoons orange juice
150 ml double cream	¼ pint double cream
3 egg whites	3 egg whites

Put the sugar in a saucepan with the water and heat gently until the sugar has dissolved, stirring. Add the fruit and cook gently for a few minutes until the juice is starting to run out. Sieve and allow to become quite cold.

Place the gelatine in a small bowl with the cold water and leave for 3 minutes to become a sponge, add orange juice. Stand the bowl in a pan of simmering water and allow the gelatine to dissolve, cool slightly and stir into the fruit purée, leave until almost set.

Whisk the cream until it forms soft peaks and stiffly whisk the egg whites. Stir the cream into the purée and fold in the egg whites. Turn into a 1¼ l (2 pint) strong, moulded glass or ovenproof dish.

To freeze: cover with a lid of foil, label and freeze.

To serve: thaw overnight in the refrigerator. If liked, the mousse may be decorated with a little whipped cream and fresh redcurrants before serving.

Pears in fresh raspberry sauce

Metric	Imperial
175 g granulated sugar	6 oz granulated sugar
600 ml water	1 pint water
6 pears	6 pears
225 g raspberries	8 oz raspberries

Cooking Time: about 25 minutes

Put the sugar and water in a shallow pan and bring slowly to the boil, stirring, until all the sugar has dissolved. Peel the pears, leaving whole with the stalks still on. Add the pears to the saucepan and arrange them on their sides so that they are almost submerged in the syrup. Bring to simmering point, cover and simmer for about 15 to 20 minutes, until tender. This will very much depend on the variety of pears used. Remove the pears and lay them in a rigid container. Sieve the raspberries and stir in enough of the sugar syrup to make a coating consistency. Spoon over the pears.

To freeze: cover, label and freeze.

To serve: thaw overnight in the refrigerator. Lift out the pears and arrange standing upright in a serving dish. Spoon the sauce over them and serve with plenty of whipped cream.

Serves 6

Easy lemon mousse

Metric	Imperial
4 eggs	4 eggs
100 g caster sugar	4 oz caster sugar
2 large lemons	2 large lemons
15 g gelatine	½ oz gelatine
3 × 15 ml spoons water	3 tablespoons water

Separate the eggs, place the yolks in a bowl with the sugar and beat until creamy. Grate the lemon rind finely, squeeze the juice from both lemons and add to the egg mixture.

Put the gelatine in a small bowl or cup with cold water and leave to stand for 3 minutes to become a sponge. Stand the bowl in a pan of simmering water and allow the gelatine to dissolve. Cool slightly and stir into the lemon mixture, leave for a few minutes until the mixture starts to set. Whisk the egg whites until stiff and fold into the lemon mixture. Put into a 1¼ l (2 pint) straight-sided, strong moulded glass or ovenproof dish.

To freeze: cover with a lid of foil, label and freeze.

To serve: remove the foil and thaw overnight in the refrigerator or for 4 hours at room temperature.

Strawberry fool; Redcurrant and raspberry mousse; Easy lemon mousse; Pears in fresh raspberry sauce

Strawberry fool

Metric	Imperial
225 g strawberries, hulled	8 oz strawberries, hulled
300 ml double cream	½ pint double cream
50 g caster sugar	2 oz caster sugar
2 × 15 ml spoons	2 tablespoons
Cointreau	Cointreau

Sieve the strawberries. Whisk the cream until thick and fold in the sugar, strawberry purée and Cointreau. Turn into four strong individual serving pots.

To freeze: cover, label and freeze.

To serve: thaw in the refrigerator for 2 to 3 hours, decorate each fool with a halved strawberry and serve with tuiles almond biscuits (see page 83).

Bramble mousse

Metric	Imperial
450 g blackberries	1 lb blackberries
100 g caster sugar	4 oz caster sugar
2 × 15 ml spoons lemon juice	2 tablespoons lemon juice
3 × 15 ml spoons cold water	3 tablespoons cold water
15 g gelatine	½ oz gelatine
150 ml double cream	¼ pint double cream
3 egg whites	3 egg whites

Cooking Time: 8 minutes.

Pick over the blackberries and place in a saucepan, with the sugar and lemon juice, over a low heat, to draw the juices and dissolve the sugar, then cover and simmer gently for about 5 minutes, or until the fruit is soft.

Place the cold water in a basin, sprinkle on the gelatine and leave to stand for 3 minutes, until it becomes a sponge. Draw the pan from the heat and add the gelatine, stir until dissolved.

Pass the fruit and juice through a sieve to make a purée, set on one side until it is cold and shows signs of setting. Whisk the cream until it forms soft peaks, stiffly whisk the egg whites, fold both into the purée until evenly blended.

To freeze: turn into a 1¼ l (2 pint) strong, moulded glass or ovenproof dish. Cover, label and freeze.

To serve: remove the cover and thaw overnight in the refrigerator, or 4 to 6 hours at room temperature. If liked, spoon into glasses, top each with a blackberry and serve with extra cream.

Fresh fruit salad

Metric	Imperial
100 g caster sugar	4 oz caster sugar
8 × 15 ml spoons water	8 tablespoons water
1 × 15 ml spoon lemon juice	1 tablespoon lemon juice
225 g large black grapes, peeled and pips removed	8 oz large black grapes, peeled and pips removed
225 g eating apples, peeled (if liked), cored and sliced	8 oz eating apples, peeled (if liked), cored and sliced
1 large orange, peeled and sliced or segmented	1 large orange, peeled and sliced or segmented
1 grapefruit, peeled and segmented	1 grapefruit, peeled and segmented
1 small honeydew melon, peeled, seeded and cut in cubes	1 small honeydew melon, peeled, seeded and cut in cubes
1 Charentais melon, peeled, seeded and cut in cubes	1 Charentais melon, peeled, seeded and cut in cubes

Buy a quantity of fruit at a local market if you have one, if not buy when prices are reasonable. Do not buy over-ripe fruits as the freezer softens the texture slightly.

Dissolve the sugar in the water over a low heat. Cool, then stir in the lemon juice. Pour into a rigid container, stir in the fruit and mix well.

To freeze: cover, label and freeze.

To serve: thaw overnight in the refrigerator. If liked, add more fruit, eg fresh strawberries or cherries, bananas and pears, and stir in 2 × 15 ml spoons (2 tablespoons) of orange liqueur.

Serves 8

Bramble mousse; Fresh fruit salad

Easy lemon cheesecake

Metric	Imperial
100 g digestive biscuits	4 oz digestive biscuits
50 g butter	2 oz butter
25 g demerara sugar	1 oz demerara sugar
225 g cream cheese	8 oz cream cheese
150 ml double cream	¼ pint double cream
Small can condensed milk	Small can condensed milk
4 × 15 ml spoons lemon juice	4 tablespoons lemon juice

Crush the biscuits with a rolling pin. Melt the butter in a pan, add the sugar then blend in the biscuit crumbs and mix well, turn into a deep 18 cm/7 inch pie plate or flan dish and press into shape around the base and sides of the plate with the back of a spoon.

Place the cream cheese in a bowl, cream until soft and beat in the cream and condensed milk. Slowly add the lemon juice. Pour the mixture into the flan case.

To freeze: cover, label and freeze.

To serve: thaw overnight in the refrigerator. Garnish with a twist of lemon.

Sharp grapefruit cheesecake

Metric	Imperial
15 g gelatine	½ oz gelatine
3 × 15 ml spoons cold water	3 tablespoons cold water
450 g cream cheese	1 lb cream cheese
170 g can concentrated unsweetened grapefruit juice, thawed	6 oz can concentrated unsweetened grapefruit juice, thawed
75 g caster sugar	3 oz caster sugar
300 ml double cream	½ pint double cream
100 g digestive biscuits	4 oz digestive biscuits
50 g butter	2 oz butter
25 g demerara sugar	1 oz demerara sugar

Place the gelatine in a small basin with the cold water and leave to stand for 5 minutes, then place in a pan of simmering water and leave to dissolve until the gelatine has become clear, remove and leave to cool. Cream the cheese until soft and gradually beat in the grapefruit juice and caster sugar. Stir in the cooled gelatine. Whisk the cream until thick but not stiff and fold into the cheesecake mixture.

Turn into a lightly oiled 20 cm (8 in) cake tin and place in the refrigerator. Crush the biscuits finely. Melt the butter in a pan and stir in the biscuit crumbs and demerara sugar, press over the cheesecake.

To freeze: cover with a lid of foil, label and freeze.

To serve: thaw overnight in the refrigerator. Turn out the cheesecake and serve either way up. If liked, decorate with whipped cream, strawberries, raspberries or grapes.

Ginger orange ring

Metric	Imperial
150 ml whipping cream	¼ pint whipping cream
225 g ginger biscuits	8 oz ginger biscuits

Whisk the cream until thick, place in a piping bag fitted with a star pipe and sandwich together the biscuits and shape into a circle. An easy way is to put them in a loose-bottomed cake tin lined with a piece of foil, with a jam jar in the centre, sloping the biscuits slightly to fit in a circle around the jar.

To freeze: open freeze, then slip the biscuit circle off the base of the cake tin, wrap in a double thickness of foil, seal, label and return to the freezer.

To serve: remove the wrapping, slip on to a serving dish and thaw in the refrigerator for 6 to 8 hours. Fill the centre with orange segments, which have been mixed with caster sugar and left to stand for at least an hour before using.

Sharp grapefruit cheesecake; Easy lemon cheesecake; Ginger orange ring

Raspberry pavlova

Metric	Imperial
3 large egg whites	3 large egg whites
175 g caster sugar	6 oz caster sugar
½ teaspoon white vinegar	½ teaspoon white vinegar
2 × 5 ml spoons cornflour	2 teaspoons cornflour

Cooking Time: 1 hour
Oven: 140°C, 275°F, Gas Mark 1

Whisk the egg whites until stiff, whisk in the sugar a spoonful at a time. Blend the vinegar with the cornflour and whisk into the egg whites with the last spoonful of sugar.

Lay a sheet of silicone paper on a baking sheet and mark a 20 cm (8 in) circle on it. Spread the meringue out to cover the circle, building up the sides to come higher than the centre.

Bake in the oven for 1 hour, then turn off the oven and leave the meringue until quite cold.

To freeze: place in a rigid container, cover, label and freeze.

To serve: place the meringue on a serving dish. Whisk 300 ml (½ pint) double cream until thick. Crush 225 g (8 oz) of raspberries to a purée and stir into the cream, pile into the centre of the meringue and decorate with 225 g (8 oz) whole fresh raspberries. Leave to stand for an hour in the refrigerator before serving.

Serves 6 to 8

Hazelnut meringue gâteau

Metric	Imperial
100 g hazelnuts	4 oz hazelnuts
4 egg whites	4 egg whites
225 g caster sugar	8 oz caster sugar
1 × 5 ml spoon white vinegar	1 teaspoon white vinegar
150 ml double cream	¼ pint double cream
40 g butter	1½ oz butter
25 g cocoa	1 oz cocoa
3 × 15 ml spoons milk	3 tablespoons milk
100 g icing sugar	4 oz icing sugar

Cooking Time: 30 minutes
Oven: 190°C, 375°F, Gas Mark 5

Place the hazelnuts on a tray and put into a moderately hot oven for a few minutes, tip on to a clean tea towel, rub them well together and the skins will flake off. Place in a blender and grind. Lightly brush the sides of two 20 cm (8 in) sandwich tins with oil and line the base with non-stick parchment.

Whisk the egg whites until stiff, whisk in half the sugar a spoonful at a time, until the meringue is glossy. Mix the ground hazelnuts with the remaining sugar and fold into the meringue with the vinegar. Divide the mixture between the tins, spread flat and bake in the lower part of a moderately hot oven for 30 minutes. Then turn off the heat and leave to cool in the oven. Remove, turn out and peel off the paper. Whisk the cream until thick. Melt the butter in a small saucepan, stir in the cocoa and cook gently for 1 minute. Stir in the milk and icing sugar. Mix well to a thick spreading consistency and spread over one half of the meringue, spread the cream on the other half and sandwich together.

To freeze: open freeze, then pack in a large rigid polythene container, cover, label and return to the freezer.

To serve: place on a serving dish and thaw for at least 12 hours in the refrigerator. Dust with a little icing sugar and decorate with chocolate curls before serving.

Serves 8

Ginger and pineapple meringue gâteau; Raspberry pavlova; Hazelnut meringue gâteau

Ginger and pineapple meringue gâteau

Metric

4 egg whites
100 g caster sugar
100 g soft brown sugar
300 ml whipping cream
248 g can crushed
pineapple, drained
2–3 pieces stem ginger,
finely chopped

Imperial

4 egg whites
4 oz caster sugar
4 oz soft brown sugar
½ pint whipping cream
8¾ oz can crushed
pineapple, drained
2–3 pieces stem ginger,
finely chopped

Cooking time: 3–4 hours
Oven: 110°C, 225°F, Gas Mark ¼

Line two large baking trays with non-stick household silicone paper or well greased greaseproof paper. On one baking tray, mark out a circle 20 cm (8 in) in diameter. On the other, mark one circle 18 cm (7 in) and another 15 cm (6 in) in diameter; use plates and saucers as guides. Whisk the egg whites with a whisk until they form peaks then add both the sugars in spoonfuls, whisking well after each addition. Divide the mixture between the marked circles and spread it out to cover.

Bake in a very cool oven for 3 to 4 hours, or until the meringues are firm to touch and dried out. Remove from the oven, leave to cool and peel off the paper. Whisk the cream until thick and fold in the pineapple and ginger. Spread half the cream on the largest piece of meringue, then cover with the next size of meringue, cover with the remaining cream and put the small meringue on top.

To freeze: open freeze, then pack in a large rigid polythene container (meringue is brittle when frozen), cover, label and return to freezer.

To serve: place on a serving dish and thaw in the refrigerator for at least 12 hours.

Serves 6 to 8

Chocolate simpkins; Chocolate and coffee torte; Special chocolate dessert cake

Chocolate simpkins

Metric

150 g plain chocolate
2 eggs, separated
50 g caster sugar
150 ml double cream
75–100 g glacé fruits,
chopped
A little Cointreau to taste

Imperial

5 oz plain chocolate
2 eggs, separated
2 oz caster sugar
$\frac{1}{4}$ pint double cream
3–4 oz glacé fruits,
chopped
A little Cointreau to taste

Break the chocolate into small pieces, place in a bowl, stand over a pan of simmering water and leave until melted. Do not allow the chocolate to get too hot. Coat the insides of 6 small, strong moulds or paper cake cases with the chocolate, using the handle of a teaspoon to make a smooth, even coating and leave to set.

Separate the eggs and whisk the yolks until well blended. Whisk the egg whites until stiff and whisk in the sugar a teaspoon at a time.

Whisk the cream until it holds soft peaks, then fold into the egg white mixture with the yolks, glacé fruits and Cointreau to taste.

Divide the mixture between the moulds and smooth the tops.

To freeze: cover each mould with a piece of foil, seal, label, and freeze at once.

To serve: thaw at room temperature for about 5 minutes, then gently ease out on to individual plates.

Serves 6

Special chocolate dessert cake

Metric

225 g milk chocolate
225 g margarine
2 eggs
25 g caster sugar
225 g Nice biscuits
Chocolate curls

Imperial

8 oz milk chocolate
8 oz margarine
2 eggs
1 oz caster sugar
8 oz Nice biscuits
Chocolate curls

This makes a special party pudding, because it looks so spectacular.
Remove the ends from two 453 g (1 lb) cans, wash and dry them thoroughly, then cover one end of each can with a double thickness piece of foil. Break the chocolate into small pieces, place in a pan with the margarine and heat gently until melted. Beat the eggs and sugar together until blended, then gradually add the chocolate mixture a little at a time. Break the biscuits into 1.5 cm ($\frac{1}{2}$ in) pieces and blend into the chocolate mixture, pack into the two tins and leave in the refrigerator for 3 to 4 hours to set.
Remove the piece of foil from the base of each can, gently press out the chocolate rolls and push firmly together.
To freeze: wrap in a double thickness of foil, seal, label and freeze.
To serve: unwrap and place on a serving dish, cover with 150 ml/$\frac{1}{4}$ pint whipped cream and decorate with piped cream and chocolate curls. Serve cut in slices.
Serves 8

Chocolate and coffee torte

Metric

75 g butter
75 g caster sugar
40 g cocoa
1 egg yolk
1 × 15 ml spoon sherry
50 g chopped hazelnuts
32 sponge finger biscuits
Generous 150 ml black coffee

Imperial

3 oz butter
3 oz caster sugar
1$\frac{1}{2}$ oz cocoa
1 egg yolk
1 tablespoon sherry
2 oz chopped hazelnuts
32 sponge finger biscuits
Generous $\frac{1}{4}$ pint black coffee

Line a 20 cm/8 inch round tin with foil. Cream the butter and sugar together until light and fluffy and then stir in the cocoa, egg yolk, sherry and nuts. Mix well together, adding a little extra sherry if necessary to make a spreading consistency.
Dip the sponge finger biscuits, sugar side down, quickly in the coffee, arrange a layer in the bottom of the tin and cover with half the chocolate filling.
Put another layer of coffee-dipped biscuits on top, spread with the remaining filling, then cover with the rest of the biscuits, coffee side uppermost.
To freeze: cover with foil, seal, label and freeze.
To serve: thaw on a serving dish in the refrigerator for 3 to 4 hours. Cover with 150 ml/$\frac{1}{4}$ pint whipped cream, decorate with small meringues and serve.
Serves 6 to 8

Plain scones

Metric	Imperial
225 g self-raising flour	8 oz self-raising flour
1 × 5 ml spoon baking powder	1 teaspoon baking powder
½ teaspoon salt	½ teaspoon salt
50 g margarine	2 oz margarine
About 150 ml milk to mix	About ¼ pint milk to mix

Cooking Time: 8–10 minutes
Oven: 230°C, 450°F, Gas Mark 8

Sieve the flour, baking powder and salt into a bowl. Rub in the margarine until the mixture resembles fine breadcrumbs. Make a well in the centre and stir in sufficient milk to make a soft dough. Turn on to a floured table and knead until smooth, then roll out to about 2 cm (¾ in) thickness. Cut into 8 rounds with a 5 cm (2 in) cutter. Place on a greased baking sheet, brush with a little milk and bake at the top of a hot oven for 8 to 10 minutes, or until a pale brown. Cool on a wire rack.

To freeze: pack in a polythene bag, seal, label and freeze. To serve: for speed, take the scones straight from the freezer and reheat in a hot oven for 10 minutes. If preferred, thaw at room temperature for 2 hours.

Makes 8 scones

Cheese scones

Metric	Imperial
225 g self-raising flour	8 oz self-raising flour
½ teaspoon salt	½ teaspoon salt
40 g margarine	1½ oz margarine
50 g Cheddar cheese, grated	2 oz Cheddar cheese, grated
25 g Parmesan cheese, grated	1 oz Parmesan cheese, grated
1 × 5 ml spoon dry mustard	1 teaspoon dry mustard
About 150 ml milk to mix	About ¼ pint milk to mix

Cooking Time: 10 minutes
Oven: 230°C, 450°F, Gas Mark 8

Sieve the flour and salt into a bowl and rub in the margarine until the mixture resembles breadcrumbs. Mix the cheeses together and stir 50 g (2 oz) into the bowl with the mustard. Add enough milk to make a soft dough. Turn on to a floured surface, knead lightly, then roll out to 2 cm (¾ in) thickness. Cut into 10 rounds with a 5 cm (2 in) cutter. Place on a greased baking sheet and sprinkle with the remaining cheese. Bake in a hot oven for 10 minutes, or until brown. Cool on a wire rack.

To freeze: pack in a polythene bag, seal, label and freeze. To serve: as Plain Scones.

Makes 10 scones

Wholemeal scones

Metric	Imperial
100 g wholemeal flour	4 oz wholemeal flour
100 g self-raising flour	4 oz self-raising flour
2 × 5 ml spoons baking powder	2 teaspoons baking powder
½ teaspoon salt	½ teaspoon salt
50 g margarine	2 oz margarine
About 150 ml milk	About ¼ pint milk

Make, bake, freeze and serve as Plain Scones.

Wholemeal scones; Plain scones; Cheese scones

Scotch pancakes

Metric	Imperial
Lard for greasing	*Lard for greasing*
100 g self-raising flour	*4 oz self-raising flour*
25 g caster sugar	*1 oz caster sugar*
1 egg	*1 egg*
150 ml milk	*¼ pint milk*

Cooking Time: 10 minutes

Prepare a heavy frying pan, or the solid hot plate of an electric cooker, by rubbing the surface with salt (on a pad of kitchen paper) and then greasing lightly with lard. When ready to cook the pancakes, heat the frying pan or hot plate until the lard is just hazy, then wipe off any fat with kitchen paper.

Put the flour and sugar in a bowl, add the egg and half the milk and beat until smooth, then beat in the remaining milk. Spoon the mixture on to the heated surface in rounds, spacing well. When bubbles rise to the surface, turn the pancakes with a palette knife and cook the other side for a further ½ to 1 minute until golden brown. Place on a wire rack to cool while cooking the remaining mixture.

To freeze: when cold, place on a flat surface and open freeze. Stack neatly together and wrap in foil, seal, label and return to the freezer.

To serve: spread on a tray, put in a cold oven and turn the heat to 200°C, 400°F, Gas Mark 6 for 10 to 15 minutes, or until warmed through. Serve while still warm, spread with butter.

Makes about 18 pancakes

Moist tacky gingerbread

Metric	Imperial
175 g plain flour	*6 oz plain flour*
2 × 5 ml spoons baking powder	*2 teaspoons baking powder*
2 × 5 ml spoons ground ginger	*2 teaspoons ground ginger*
½ teaspoon mixed spice	*½ teaspoon mixed spice*
Pinch of salt	*Pinch of salt*
50 g butter	*2 oz butter*
50 g brown sugar	*2 oz brown sugar*
1 × 15 ml spoon black treacle	*1 tablespoon black treacle*
1 × 15 ml spoon golden syrup	*1 tablespoon golden syrup*
1 × 5 ml spoon bicarbonate of soda	*1 teaspoon bicarbonate of soda*
225 ml warm milk	*7 fl oz warm milk*
2 eggs, beaten	*2 eggs, beaten*
40 g stem ginger, finely chopped	*1½ oz stem ginger, finely chopped*

Cooking Time: 40–50 minutes
Oven: 160°C, 325°F, Gas Mark 3

Grease a 20 cm (8 in) square tin and line it with greased greaseproof paper.

Sieve the flour, baking powder, spices and salt into a bowl. Cream the butter with the sugar and treacle and syrup and beat well. Dissolve the bicarbonate of soda in the milk and stir into the creamed mixture with the flour, beaten eggs and ginger. Beat well and pour into the tin.

Bake in a warm oven for 40 to 50 minutes until well risen. Leave to cool in the tin.

To freeze: wrap in foil, seal, label and freeze.

To serve: unwrap and leave to thaw at room temperature for 3 to 4 hours. If liked, this cake could be iced with a lemon icing.

Scotch pancakes; Moist tacky gingerbread; Homemade brown bread

Homemade brown bread

Metric

450 ml hand-hot water
1 × 5 ml spoon sugar
15 g dried yeast

Dough:
350 g strong plain flour
350 g wholemeal flour
2 × 5 ml spoons sugar
2–3 × 5 ml spoons salt
1 × 15 ml spoon
vegetable oil
Milk to glaze
A little cracked wheat

Imperial

¾ pint hand-hot water
1 teaspoon sugar
½ oz dried yeast

Dough:
12 oz strong plain flour
12 oz wholemeal flour
2 teaspoons sugar
2–3 teaspoons salt
1 tablespoon
vegetable oil
Milk to glaze
A little cracked wheat

Cooking Time: 30–40 minutes
Oven: 230°C, 450°F, Gas Mark 8

Make the yeast liquid by mixing the water and sugar and stirring in the dried yeast. Leave for 10 to 15 minutes until frothy.

Put all the dry ingredients in a bowl. Pour on the yeast mixture and the oil and mix with a fork, then knead until smooth and no longer sticky, about 10 minutes. Grease a polythene bag with half a teaspoon of vegetable oil, put in the dough and leave to rise in a warm place, until doubled in bulk; this will take about an hour at room temperature. Knead until it returns to its original bulk. Shape it and put it in a greased 1 kg (2 lb) loaf tin. Glaze with milk and sprinkle with a little cracked wheat, cover with an oiled bag and leave to rise in a warm place until the dough has reached the top of the tin.

Remove the bag and bake in a hot oven for 30 to 40 minutes, or until the loaf is evenly browned and sounds hollow when tapped on the bottom.

To freeze: cool, wrap in a double thickness of foil or in a polythene bag, seal, label and freeze.

To serve: thaw for 3 to 4 hours at room temperature or overnight in the refrigerator.

Orange fruit teabread

Date and walnut cake

Metric	Imperial
300 ml boiling water	½ pint boiling water
225 g dates, chopped	8 oz dates, chopped
1 × 5 ml spoon	1 teaspoon
bicarbonate of soda	bicarbonate of soda
225 g caster sugar	8 oz caster sugar
75 g butter	3 oz butter
1 egg, beaten	1 egg, beaten
275 g plain flour	10 oz plain flour
1 × 5 ml spoon baking	1 teaspoon baking
powder	powder
½ teaspoon salt	½ teaspoon salt
50 g walnuts, chopped	2 oz walnuts, chopped

For the Topping:

65 g brown sugar	2½ oz brown sugar
25 g butter	1 oz butter
2 × 15 ml spoons milk	2 tablespoons milk
Walnut halves	Walnut halves

Cooking Time: 1 hour
Oven: 180°C, 350°F, Gas Mark 4

Grease a 23 cm (9 in) square tin and line it with greased greaseproof paper. Put the water, dates and bicarbonate of soda in a bowl and leave to stand for 5 minutes. Cream the sugar and butter together until soft then stir in the egg with the water and dates. Sieve the flour with the baking powder and salt and fold in with the walnuts. Turn into the tin and smooth the top.
Bake in a moderate oven for 1 hour. Turn out and leave to cool on a wire rack.
Place all the topping ingredients, except the walnuts, in a pan and boil for 3 minutes, then spread over the cake. Decorate with walnut halves, and leave to set.
To freeze: wrap in a double thickness of foil, seal, label and freeze.
To serve: unwrap and thaw at room temperature for 5 to 6 hours.

Apricot fruit cake

Metric	Imperial
200 g self-raising flour	7 oz self-raising flour
Pinch of salt	Pinch of salt
100 g glacé cherries	4 oz glacé cherries
425 g can apricots	15 oz can apricots
150 g butter	5 oz butter
115 g caster sugar	4½ oz caster sugar
2 large eggs, beaten	2 large eggs, beaten
2 × 15 ml spoons milk	2 tablespoons milk
100 g sultanas	4 oz sultanas
100 g raisins	4 oz raisins
100 g currants	4 oz currants

Cooking Time: 2 hours
Oven: 160°C, 325°F, Gas Mark 3

Grease and line a 1½ kg (3 lb) loaf tin with greased greaseproof paper. Sieve the salt and flour together. Halve the cherries, roll three-quarters of them in flour and keep the remainder for topping. Drain the apricots and chop finely. Cream the butter and sugar until light and creamy. Beat in the eggs, adding a tablespoon of flour with the last amount of egg. Fold in the flour, milk and all the fruit, except the cherries for the topping. Turn into the prepared tin and arrange the cherries on the top. Bake in a warm oven for 2 hours, or until cooked. Leave to cool in the tin.
To freeze: remove the paper and wrap in a double thickness of foil, seal, label and freeze.
To serve: unwrap and thaw at room temperature for about 6 hours.
Note: this is a very moist fruit cake and should be kept in the fridge wrapped in foil rather than in a cake tin.

Orange fruit teabread

Metric	Imperial
150 g currants	*5 oz currants*
150 g sultanas	*5 oz sultanas*
150 g brown sugar	*5 oz brown sugar*
Finely grated rind of 2 oranges	*Finely grated rind of 2 oranges*
300 ml hot tea	*½ pint hot tea*
275 g self-raising flour	*10 oz self-raising flour*
1 egg	*1 egg*

Cooking Time: 1½ hours
Oven: 150°C, 300°F, Gas Mark 2

Put the fruit, sugar and orange rind in a bowl, pour over the hot tea, stir well, cover and leave to stand overnight. Grease and line with greased greaseproof paper a 20 cm (8 in) round cake tin. Stir the flour and egg into the fruit mixture and mix thoroughly.

Turn the mixture into the tin and bake in a cool oven for 1½ hours.

Leave to cool on a wire rack.

To freeze: wrap in a double thickness of foil, seal, label and freeze.

To serve: thaw at room temperature for 4 to 5 hours and serve either sliced with butter or just as it is.

Date and walnut cake; Apricot fruit cake

75

Simnel cake

Metric	Imperial
175 g butter, softened	6 oz butter, softened
175 g soft brown sugar	6 oz soft brown sugar
3 eggs	3 eggs
175 g plain flour	6 oz plain flour
3 × 5 ml spoons mixed spice	3 teaspoons mixed spice
1 × 5 ml spoon baking powder	1 teaspoon baking powder
2 × 15 ml spoons milk	2 tablespoons milk
275 g mixed dried fruit	10 oz mixed dried fruit
50 g glacé cherries, chopped	2 oz glacé cherries, chopped
25 g mixed cut peel, chopped	1 oz mixed cut peel, chopped
Finely grated rind of 1 lemon	Finely grated rind of 1 lemon
50 g ground almonds	2 oz ground almonds

Decoration:	Decoration:
450 g almond paste	1 lb almond paste
1 × 15 ml spoon sieved apricot jam	1 tablespoon sieved apricot jam
1 egg white	1 egg white
Foil-wrapped Easter eggs	Foil-wrapped Easter eggs

Cooking Time: 2½ hours
Oven: 150°C, 300°F, Gas Mark 2
220°C, 425°F, Gas Mark 7

Grease a round 18 cm (7 in) cake tin and line it with greased greaseproof paper. Put all the cake ingredients together in a large mixing bowl and beat together with a wooden spoon until well blended – this will take 2 to 3 minutes. Place half the mixture in the tin and smooth the top. Roll one-third of the almond paste to fit the tin and place on top of the cake mixture. Put the remaining mixture in tin and smooth the top.

Bake in a cool oven for 2½ hours, or until cooked, then leave to cool on a wire rack. Brush the top of the cake with the apricot jam. Roll out one-third of the remaining almond paste to an 18 cm (7 in) round and place on the cake, pinching the edges. Roll out the remaining paste, shape into 11 balls and arrange them around the edge of the cake. If liked, brush with a little beaten egg white and bake at 220°C, 425°F, Gas Mark 7 for 2 to 3 minutes to brown the almond paste lightly. Cool and decorate with Easter eggs.

To freeze: open freeze, then put in a large foil container, cover, label and freeze.

To serve: thaw at room temperature for 6 to 8 hours.

Christmas cake

Metric	Imperial
250 g plain flour	9 oz plain flour
¼ teaspoon salt	¼ teaspoon salt
1 × 5 ml spoon mixed spice	1 teaspoon mixed spice
225 g butter	8 oz butter
225 g soft brown sugar	8 oz soft brown sugar
1 × 15 ml spoon black treacle	1 tablespoon black treacle
4 eggs	4 eggs
1 kg mixed dried fruit	2 lb mixed dried fruit
100 g glacé cherries, quartered	4 oz glacé cherries, quartered
100 g candied mixed peel, chopped	4 oz candied mixed peel, chopped
50 g almonds, blanched and chopped	2 oz almonds, blanched and chopped
2 × 15 ml spoons brandy	2 tablespoons brandy

Cooking Time: 4 hours
Oven: 150°C, 300°F, Gas Mark 2
  120°C, 250°F, Gas Mark ½

Line a 20 cm (8 in) diameter cake tin with a double thickness of greased greaseproof paper. Sieve together the flour, salt and spice. Cream the butter and sugar until light and beat in the treacle. Add the eggs one at a time, beating well after each addition and adding a spoonful of flour with each egg. Fold in the remaining flour. Add the dried fruit, cherries, peel and almonds and mix well. Place in the tin and make a hollow in the centre.

Bake the cake in a cool oven for 3 hours, then reduce the oven temperature and bake for a further hour, or until cooked. Cover the cake with a piece of brown paper if it is becoming too brown. Leave to cool in the tin for 20 minutes, then turn out, pierce with a skewer and spoon the brandy over the top and leave to cool.

To freeze: wrap in double thickness foil, seal, label and freeze.

To serve: thaw at room temperature for 6 to 8 hours.

Note: rich fruit cake improves with freezing. Thaw and ice this cake a week or so before Christmas.

Simnel cake; Christmas cake

Devil's food cake

Devil's food cake

Metric	Imperial
90 g plain flour	3½ oz plain flour
1 × 15 ml spoon cocoa	1 tablespoon cocoa
½ teaspoon	½ teaspoon
bicarbonate of soda	bicarbonate of soda
½ teaspoon baking	½ teaspoon baking
powder	powder
65 g caster sugar	2½ oz caster sugar
1 × 15 ml spoon golden	1 tablespoon golden
syrup	syrup
1 egg, beaten	1 egg, beaten
6 × 15 ml spoons salad	6 tablespoons salad
or corn oil	or corn oil
6 × 15 ml spoons milk	6 tablespoons milk

Cooking Time: 30–35 minutes
Oven: 160°C, 325°F, Gas Mark 3

Grease two 18 cm (7 in) sandwich tins and line with greased greaseproof paper. Sieve the flour, cocoa, bicarbonate of soda and baking powder into a mixing bowl. Make a well in the centre and add the sugar and syrup. Gradually stir in the egg, oil and milk and beat well to make a smooth batter.

Pour into the tins and bake in a warm oven for 30 to 35 minutes, or until the tops spring back when lightly pressed with a finger.

Turn out and leave to cool on a wire rack. Sandwich together with American Frosting (see page 84) and spread the remainder over the top and sides.

To freeze: open freeze, then place in a polythene bag, seal label and return to the freezer.

To serve: remove the bag, place the cake on a plate and thaw at room temperature for about 4½ hours.

Chocolate fudge cake

Chocolate fudge cake

Metric	Imperial
100 g plain chocolate	4 oz plain chocolate
300 ml milk	½ pint milk
100 g demerara sugar	4 oz demerara sugar
1 × 5 ml spoon	1 teaspoon
bicarbonate of soda	bicarbonate of soda
100 g butter	4 oz butter
100 g caster sugar	4 oz caster sugar
2 eggs, separated	2 eggs, separated
225 g plain flour, sieved	8 oz plain flour, sieved

Icing:	Icing:
115 g butter	4½ oz butter
75 g cocoa, sieved	3 oz cocoa, sieved
Scant 150 ml milk	Scant ¼ pint milk
350 g icing sugar, sieved	12 oz icing sugar, sieved

Cooking Time: 45 minutes
Oven: 180°C, 350°F, Gas Mark 4

Grease two 20 cm (8 in) sandwich tins and line them with greased greaseproof paper. Melt the chocolate in a saucepan with the milk and demerara sugar until dissolved, but do not allow it to boil. Remove from the heat, add the bicarbonate of soda and leave to cool. In a separate bowl, cream the butter with the caster sugar and beat in the egg yolks. Whisk the egg whites until stiff. Add by degrees the chocolate mixture and the flour to the creamed mixture, and lastly fold in the egg whites. Turn into the tins and bake in a moderate oven for 45 minutes, turn out and leave to cool. To make the icing, melt the butter in a small pan, stir in the cocoa and cook gently for 1 minute. Remove the pan from the heat, stir in the icing sugar and sufficient milk to give a smooth, thick pouring consistency. Mix well and use to sandwich the cake together and pour the remaining icing over the cake. Leave to set.

To freeze: wrap in foil, seal, label and freeze.

To serve: thaw at room temperature for 5 to 6 hours. If liked, decorate with walnuts.

79

Basic Victoria sandwich

Metric	Imperial
175 g butter	6 oz butter
175 g castor sugar, warmed in the oven	6 oz caster sugar, warmed in the oven
3 eggs at room temperature	3 eggs at room temperature
175 g self-raising flour	6 oz self-raising flour

Cooking Time: 20–25 minutes
Oven: 190°C, 375°F, Gas Mark 5

This is one of the most useful standbys you can have in a freezer. It can take so many different fillings and toppings, can be eaten as cake or as a dessert, and makes a good partner for fruit. You can also vary the basic recipe by adding different flavourings. I give eight suggestions below.

Grease two 20 cm (8 in) sandwich tins and line them with greased greaseproof paper. Cream the butter and sugar together until light and fluffy. Beat the eggs and blend into the mixture, stirring in a spoonful of flour with the last egg. Sieve in the remaining flour and turn into the two tins. Bake the cakes in a moderately hot oven for 20 to 25 minutes, or until the tops spring back when lightly pressed with the fingertips. Turn out on to a wire rack and cool.

To freeze: wrap in foil, seal, label and freeze.

To serve: thaw at room temperature for 4 to 5 hours, sandwich together with whipped cream and raspberry jam, and sprinkle thickly with sifted icing sugar.

Variations on Victoria sponge

Orange and lemon sandwich
Add the finely grated rind of 1 orange or lemon to the creamed mixture.

Chocolate sandwich
Replace 25 g (1 oz) flour with 25 g (1 oz) cocoa.

Coffee sandwich
Dissolve 1 × 5 ml heaped spoon (1 heaped teaspoon) instant coffee powder in the beaten eggs before adding to the mixture.

Cherry
Add 50 g (2 oz) halved glacé cherries to the mixture before adding in the flour.

Coconut
Add 50 g (2 oz) desiccated coconut and 1 × 15 ml spoon (1 tablespoon) milk with the flour.

Queen cakes
Add 50 g (2 oz) dried fruit and a few drops vanilla essence, and bake in small tins or cake cases for 15 to 20 minutes.

Butterfly cakes
Bake in small tins or cake cases. Cut a slice from the top of each cake and cut in half, spoon or pipe a little butter cream into the centre of each cake, place the cake wings in the butter icing and dust with a little icing sugar.

Coffee walnut sandwich
To coffee mixture fold in 50 g (2 oz) chopped walnuts with the flour and when cold fill and ice with coffee butter cream.

Note: all these flavours freeze well. If liked, the sandwich can be frozen filled with cream or butter cream – but not with jam, as this tends to make the cake soggy.

Victoria sandwich

Lemon dairy sponge

Lemon dairy sponge

Metric

3 eggs
75 g .caster sugar
75 g self-raising flour
150 ml double cream
2 × 15 ml spoons lemon
curd

Imperial

3 eggs
3 oz caster sugar
3 oz self-raising flour
¼ pint double cream
2 tablespoons lemon
curd

Cooking Time: 20 minutes
Oven: 190°C, 375°F, Gas Mark 5

Grease two 18 cm (7 in) sandwich tins and line them with greased greaseproof paper. Put the eggs and sugar in a heatproof bowl over a pan of hot water and whisk until the mixture is thick, white and creamy and the whisk leaves a trail when lifted. Remove from the heat and whisk for a further 2 minutes. Sieve in the flour and carefully fold it in. Divide the mixture between the tins and bake in a moderately hot oven for 20 minutes, or until the tops spring back when lightly pressed with the fingertips. Turn on to a wire rack to cool. Whisk the cream until thick and blend in the lemon curd. Sandwich the cooled cakes with the lemon cream mixture.

To freeze: wrap in foil and a polythene bag, seal, label and freeze.

To serve: thaw overnight in the refrigerator or for 4 hours at room temperature, unwrap and sprinkle with sugar.

Tuiles almond biscuits

Tuiles almond biscuits

Metric	Imperial
65 g butter	2½ oz butter
50 g caster sugar	2 oz caster sugar
40 g plain flour	1½ oz plain flour
40 g flaked almonds	1½ oz flaked almonds

Cooking Time: 8–10 minutes
Oven: 180°C, 350°F, Gas Mark 4

Cream the butter and sugar until pale and stir in the flour and almonds. Form into marble-sized balls and place half of them about 7.5 cm (3 in) apart on a well greased baking sheet. Flatten with a damp fork and bake in a moderate oven for 8 to 10 minutes, until a pale golden brown.

Remove the baking sheet from the oven and leave for a few seconds. The biscuits are very thin and brittle, so lift them off the baking sheet carefully with a palette knife, lay on a lightly oiled rolling pin and leave to harden. Repeat with the remaining mixture.

To freeze: pack carefully into a rigid container, cover, label and freeze.

To serve: thaw at room temperature for about an hour. Serve with mousses and fools.

Makes about 18

Note: these lose flavour quickly in a cake tin, but will keep if in the freezer.

Ginger spice cake

Metric	Imperial
100 g margarine	4 oz margarine
175 g golden syrup	6 oz golden syrup
50 g black treacle	2 oz black treacle
50 g brown sugar	2 oz brown sugar
150 ml milk	¼ pint milk
2 eggs	2 eggs
225 g plain flour	8 oz plain flour
2 × 5 ml spoons mixed spice	2 teaspoons mixed spice
2 × 5 ml spoons ground ginger	2 teaspoons ground ginger
1 × 5 ml spoon bicarbonate of soda	1 teaspoon bicarbonate of soda
100 g sultanas	4 oz sultanas

Cooking Time: ¾ to 1 hour
Oven: 160°C, 325°F, Gas Mark 3

Grease a 20 cm (8 in) square cake tin and line it with greased greaseproof paper. Warm together the margarine, syrup, treacle and sugar, add the milk and allow to cool. Beat the eggs and blend with the cooled mixture. Sieve the dry ingredients together, add the cooled mixture and the sultanas, folding in with a spoon. Turn into the tin and bake in a warm oven for ¾ to 1 hour, or until well risen and golden brown. Turn out and leave to cool on a wire rack.
To freeze: wrap in foil, seal, label and freeze.
To serve: thaw at room temperature for 5 to 6 hours.

American frosting

Metric	Imperial
225 g granulated sugar	8 oz granulated sugar
150 ml water	¼ pint water
Pinch of cream of tartar	Pinch of cream of tartar
1 egg white, whisked	1 egg white, whisked

This is a good icing to use on cakes you are freezing. Put the sugar into a saucepan with the water and stir over a low heat until the sugar has dissolved. Bring to the boil and heat to 238°F, or until a small amount dropped in a saucer of cold water forms a ball. Remove from the heat, add the cream of tartar and beat lightly, until the syrup is just cloudy. Pour on to the stiffly whisked egg white, whisking all the time, and continue whisking until the mixture thickens and loses its shiny look. Use at once.

Ginger spice cake

Rich chocolate sauce

Metric

40 g butter
25 g cocoa, sieved
small can evaporated milk
100 g icing sugar, sieved

Imperial

1½ oz butter
1 oz cocoa, sieved
small can evaporated milk
4 oz icing sugar, sieved

Melt the butter in a small saucepan, stir in the cocoa and cook for 1 minute. Remove from the heat, stir in the evaporated milk and icing sugar and mix well.
To freeze: turn into a rigid polythene container, leave to cool, cover, label and freeze.
To serve: thaw at room temperature for 2 hours. Serve as a sauce with plain sponge cake, or over small choux pastry buns filled with whipped cream. It is also very good served over portions of ice-cream.

American frosting; Rich chocolate sauce

Chocolate fork biscuits

Metric	Imperial
225 g butter	8 oz butter
100 g caster sugar	4 oz caster sugar
1 × 5 ml spoon vanilla essence	1 teaspoon vanilla essence
225 g self-raising flour	8 oz self-raising flour
50 g drinking chocolate	2 oz drinking chocolate
Icing sugar and nuts (optional)	Icing sugar and nuts (optional)

Cream the butter with the sugar and vanilla essence, then work in the flour and chocolate. Divide into pieces the size of a walnut and roll into balls, place on a baking sheet and flatten with a large fork dipped in cold water.

To freeze: open freeze, then pack into a rigid container, cover, label and freeze.

To cook: take straight from the freezer, place on a greased baking tray and bake in a moderately hot oven (190°C, 375°F, Gas Mark 5) for 12 to 15 minutes. Leave to firm for a minute on the baking tray, then cool on a wire rack. Decorate with icing sugar and nuts, if liked.

Makes about 36 biscuits

Chocolate crunch biscuits; Demerara biscuits

Chocolate fork biscuits

Chocolate crunch biscuits

Metric

200 g plain flour
25 g cocoa
Pinch salt
175 g butter
100 g caster sugar
25 g granulated sugar

Imperial

7 oz plain flour
1 oz cocoa
Pinch salt
6 oz butter
4 oz caster sugar
1 oz granulated sugar

Cooking Time: 20 minutes
Oven: 160°C, 325°F, Gas Mark 3

Sieve the flour and cocoa into a bowl with the salt. Cream the butter until soft, add the caster sugar and beat until light and fluffy, then blend in the flour and work until smooth. Divide the mixture into two equal pieces each 15 cm (6 in) long. Roll in the granulated sugar, then wrap in foil and chill in the refrigerator until firm. Grease two baking sheets, cut each roll into 16 slices, place on the baking sheets and bake in a warm oven for 20 minutes, or until the edges are turning a deeper shade of brown. Leave to cool on a wire rack.

To freeze: pack in a rigid container, cover, label and freeze.
To serve: remove from the container, thaw at room temperature for about 1 hour.
Makes 32 biscuits

Demerara biscuits

Metric

225 g plain flour
Pinch salt
175 g butter
150 g demerara sugar

Imperial

8 oz plain flour
Pinch salt
6 oz butter
5 oz demerara sugar

Cooking Time: 20 minutes
Oven: 160°C, 325°F, Gas Mark 3

Sieve the flour and salt into a bowl. Cream the butter until soft and then add 100 g (4 oz) of the sugar and beat until light and fluffy. Blend in the flour and work until smooth. Divide the mixture into two equal pieces and roll out to form sausages each 15 cm (6 in) long. Roll in the remaining sugar, then wrap in foil and chill in the refrigerator until firm. Grease two baking sheets, cut each sausage into 16 slices and place on the baking sheets. Bake in a warm oven for 20 minutes, or until the biscuits are pale golden brown at the edges. Leave to cool on a wire rack.

To freeze: pack in a rigid container, cover, label and freeze.
To serve: remove from the container, thaw at room temperature for about 1 hour.
Makes 32 biscuits

SWEETS
Coconut ice

Metric

675 g granulated sugar
300 ml water
2 pinches of cream of tartar
225 g desiccated coconut
a little pink colouring

Imperial

1½ lb granulated sugar
½ pint water
2 pinches of cream of tartar
8 oz desiccated coconut
a little pink colouring

Cooking Time: about 20 minutes

Line an 18 cm (7 in) square tin with greaseproof paper. Dissolve half the sugar in half the water, add one pinch of cream of tartar, bring to the boil and boil to 238°F, or until a little of the syrup forms a soft ball when dropped into cold water. Remove from the heat and stir in half the coconut all at once. Pour into the prepared tin and leave to set. Make a second quantity of coconut ice in the same way but, when adding the coconut, stir in a little pink colouring, avoiding over mixing. Spread over the first layer in the tin. When cold, cut in blocks and wrap in wax paper.
To freeze: overwrap in foil, seal, label and freeze.
To serve: thaw at room temperature for 5 to 6 hours.

Coconut ice

Sultana fudge

Metric	Imperial
Small can evaporated milk	Small can evaporated milk
75 g butter	3 oz butter
450 g granulated sugar	1 lb granulated sugar
150 ml water	¼ pint water
¼ teaspoon vanilla essence	¼ teaspoon vanilla essence
50 g sultanas	2 oz sultanas

Cooking Time: about 15 minutes

Butter a shallow 18 cm (7 in) square tin. Put the evaporated milk, butter, sugar and water in a heavy pan, heat slowly until the sugar has dissolved, without boiling. Boil steadily to 237°F, stirring constantly, or until a small amount forms a soft ball when dropped into cold water. Remove from heat and add vanilla essence. Cool slightly and then beat, as the mixture thickens. Stir in the sultanas as it starts to crystallise on the spoon.

Pour into the tin and leave to set. When firm, cut into 36 squares.

To freeze: pack in a rigid polythene container, cover, label and freeze.

To serve: remove from container, thaw in a single layer at room temperature for 1 to 2 hours.

Note: fudge makes a good Christmas present to give by hand – postage is out of the question as it is heavy stuff! Make ahead and freeze and it will certainly save time.

Sultana fudge

Some of the ingredients for Easy Seville orange marmalade

Easy Seville orange marmalade

Metric

$1\frac{1}{2}$ *kg frozen Seville oranges*
$1\frac{3}{4}$ *litres water*
4×15 *ml spoons lemon juice*
Scant 3 kg granulated sugar, warmed

Imperial

3 lb frozen Seville oranges
3 pints water
4 tablespoons lemon juice
6 lb granulated sugar, warmed

Cooking Time: about 40 minutes

This marmalade is made from whole fruit in a pressure cooker and is an ideal way to use frozen Seville oranges. If you haven't a large pressure cooker, make half the quantity. The time to freeze oranges is between December and February – freeze them whole and use them for marmalade before the next season comes round.

Put frozen oranges (do not thaw) and the water in the pressure cooker, cover and bring to 15 lb pressure for 20 minutes. Cool the pan in water to release the lid. Test the oranges for tenderness by pricking the skin with a pin. If it goes in easily the oranges are ready. Lift all the fruit out into a colander (catch any juice in a bowl underneath and return to the pan). Cut the oranges in half, remove all the pips and put the pips back into the pan, cover and bring to 15 lb pressure for a further 5 minutes.

Meanwhile, slice all the orange peel shells, using a knife and fork on a wooden board, put this peel, lemon juice and warmed sugar in a large preserving pan, strain in water and juice from the pressure cooker and throw away the pips, stir over the heat to dissolve the sugar, then boil rapidly. Test for setting after 10 minutes. To do this, spoon a small amount on to a cold saucer – when it is cool, the skin that forms should wrinkle when pushed with the finger. Pour into hot clean jars, cover and label.

Makes 5 kg (10 lb) marmalade.

Freezer mincemeat

Freezer mincemeat

Metric

675 g stoned raisins
100 g mixed peel
1 kg cooking apples
325 g currants
225 g sultanas
175 g shredded suet
½ teaspoon mixed spice
4 × 15 ml spoons lemon juice
Finely grated rind of 2 lemons
675 g granulated sugar
6 × 15 ml spoons rum, brandy or sherry

Imperial

1½ lb stoned raisins
4 oz mixed peel
2 lb cooking apples
12 oz currants
8 oz sultanas
6 oz shredded suet
½ teaspoon mixed spice
4 tablespoons lemon juice
Finely grated rind of 2 lemons
1½ lb granulated sugar
6 tablespoons rum, brandy or sherry

Finely chop or mince the raisins and peel. Peel, core and chop, grate or mince the apples. Place the raisins and apples in a large bowl with the other fruit, suet and spice. Add the lemon juice and rind, sugar, and rum, brandy or sherry. Mix thoroughly and leave to stand overnight.

To freeze: turn into a large rigid container or, if preferred, several small ones. Cover, label and freeze.

To serve: thaw in the refrigerator overnight and use as required.

Note: this mincemeat needs to be kept in the freezer. Because of its high proportion of apple, it will not keep for more than a month in the larder.

Egg and chive sandwiches

Metric	Imperial
3 large eggs	3 large eggs
15 g butter	½ oz butter
6 × 15 ml spoons milk	6 tablespoons milk
3 × 5 ml spoons salad cream	3 teaspoons salad cream
2 × 5 ml spoons chopped chives	2 teaspoons chopped chives
Salt and freshly ground black pepper	Salt and freshly ground black pepper

Scramble the eggs with butter and milk, leave to cool and stir in the salad cream and chives. Season well.

Cream cheese and shrimp sandwiches

Metric	Imperial
225 g cream cheese	8 oz cream cheese
50 g chopped shrimps	2 oz chopped shrimps
Salt and freshly ground black pepper	Salt and freshly ground black pepper

Combine the cheese and shrimps. Season well.

Sardine and tomato sandwiches

Metric	Imperial
175 g sardines, drained	6 oz sardines, drained
2 tomatoes	2 tomatoes
Salt and freshly ground black pepper	Salt and freshly ground black pepper

Blend the sardines with the chopped tomatoes, season well.

To freeze the sandwiches: use the fillings to make the sandwiches, then pack in layers with pieces of greaseproof paper in between. Wrap in foil.
To serve: thaw at room temperature in the foil wrapping for 4 hours and garnish as desired.

Black bread

Metric	Imperial
Yeast Mixture:	Yeast Mixture:
5 ml spoon sugar	1 teaspoon sugar
300 ml hand hot water	½ pint hand hot water
25 g dried yeast	1 oz dried yeast
Dough:	Dough:
350 g rye flour	12 oz rye flour
350 g strong white flour	12 oz strong white flour
5 ml spoon salt	1 teaspoon salt
1 × 15 ml spoon black treacle	1 tablespoon black treacle
150 ml warm milk	¼ pint milk
½ teaspoon caraway seeds	½ teaspoon caraway seeds
½ teaspoon vegetable oil	½ teaspoon vegetable oil

Cooking Time: 35–40 minutes
Oven: 220°C, 425°F, Gas Mark 7

To make up the yeast mixture, add sugar to water, sprinkle yeast on top. Stir well, leave 10–15 minutes, until frothy. To make up the dough, sieve the flours and salt into a bowl. Add the treacle to the milk and warm slightly, then add the caraway seeds to the flour, make a well in the centre and add the milk and treacle and the yeast mixture. Mix to a firm dough, put on a board, knead about 10 minutes.
Put into a polythene bag greased with ½ teaspoon vegetable oil and leave in a warm place until doubled in bulk, this will take about 1 hour at room temperature. Knead back to original bulk; this is called knocking back.
Divide the dough into 2 pieces and mould into 2 long loaves. Place on a well greased baking sheet, cover with oiled bags and leave to rise for about 40 minutes. Remove bags, brush with milk and bake for 35–40 minutes until browned and hollow sounding when tapped on base. Cool.
To freeze: wrap in a double thickness of foil or in a polythene bag, seal, label and freeze.
To serve: thaw at room temperature for 3 to 4 hours.

Sandwiches for the freezer: Egg and chive; Cream cheese and shrimp; Sardine and tomato. Black bread

Lemon sausage thyme stuffing

Metric	Imperial
25 g butter	1 oz butter
2 onions, peeled and finely chopped	2 onions, peeled and finely chopped
450 g pork sausagemeat	1 lb pork sausagemeat
225 g fresh white breadcrumbs	8 oz fresh white breadcrumbs
2–3 × 15 ml spoons finely chopped parsley	2–3 tablespoons finely chopped parsley
1 × 5 ml spoon fresh thyme, preferably lemon thyme, or ½ teaspoon dried thyme	1 teaspoon fresh thyme, preferably lemon thyme, or ½ teaspoon dried thyme
Finely grated rind of 1 lemon	Finely grated rind of 1 lemon
2 × 15 ml spoons lemon juice	2 tablespoons lemon juice
1 × 5 ml spoon salt	1 teaspoon salt
Finely ground black pepper	Finely ground black pepper
1 egg, beaten	1 egg, beaten

Cooking Time: about 10 minutes

Melt the butter in a pan, add the onion and fry until soft, about 10 minutes. Stir in the remaining ingredients and mix well together.

To freeze: put in a polythene bag, seal, label and freeze.

To serve: thaw in the refrigerator overnight, then use to stuff a turkey.

Makes enough to stuff a 5½ kg (12 lb) turkey.

Note: fresh herbs give this stuffing a much better flavour than dried ones.

Croûtons

Cut slices of white bread, remove the crusts and cut into 1.5 cm (½ in) cubes. Fry in shallow or deep fat until crisp and golden. Drain thoroughly on kitchen paper.

To freeze: pack in polythene bags, seal, label and freeze.

To serve: place uncovered, but still frozen, in a moderately hot oven (200°C, 400°F, Gas Mark 6) for about 5 minutes.

Mint sauce

Metric	Imperial
Large bunch of mint, finely chopped	Large bunch of mint, finely chopped
225 g granulated sugar	8 oz granulated sugar
300 ml water	½ pint water

Divide the mint among the sections of an ice-cube tray. Place the sugar and water in a saucepan and heat gently until the sugar has dissolved, then boil gently for 3 to 4 minutes. Pour over the mint in the ice tray. Cool.

To freeze: open freeze until solid, then remove cubes from tray and put in a polythene bag, seal, label and return to freezer.

To serve: thaw the number of cubes required in a sauce boat and add a little vinegar to taste.

Brandy butter

Metric	Imperial
175 g unsalted butter	6 oz unsalted butter
350 g icing sugar, sieved	12 oz icing sugar, sieved
4–6 × 15 ml spoons brandy	4–6 tablespoons brandy

Cream the butter with a wooden spoon until it is soft. Gradually beat in the icing sugar and continue beating until the mixture is light and soft. Beat in the brandy.

To freeze: turn into a small rigid container, cover, label and freeze.

To serve: thaw for 12 hours at room temperature, turn into a small serving dish.

Chestnut stuffing; Brandy butter; Croûtons; Lemon sausage thyme stuffing; Mint sauce

Chestnut stuffing

Metric

440 g can whole chestnuts in water, drained and chopped
100 g fresh brown breadcrumbs
Finely grated rind of ½ lemon
1 large egg, beaten
50 g butter
1 onion, peeled and chopped
Salt and freshly ground black pepper

Imperial

15½ oz can whole chestnuts in water, drained and chopped
4 oz fresh brown breadcrumbs
Finely grated rind of ½ lemon
1 large egg, beaten
2 oz butter
1 onion, peeled and chopped
Salt and freshly ground black pepper

Cooking Time: about 10 minutes

Place the chestnuts in a bowl with the breadcrumbs, lemon rind and beaten egg. Melt the butter in a small pan, add the onion and cook gently for about 10 minutes or until soft. Add to the bowl with the seasoning and mix well.
To freeze: turn into a polythene bag, seal, label and freeze.
To serve: thaw in the refrigerator overnight and then use to stuff a turkey.
Makes enough for a 5½ kg (12 lb) turkey.

Index